"Fr. Reed offers us, in the example of the saints, encouraging and inspiring ways to respond to the call to renew the face of the earth."

Cardinal Donald Wuerl
Archbishop of Washington

"Robert Reed's new book is a real gem. Using the insights of the saints and great spiritual masters, he helps readers understand what it means to live out our Christian faith, and even better, *how* to live out that faith. Let Fr. Reed, a talented evangelist and compassionate priest, guide you gently to a fuller Christian life and a deeper relationship with God."

James Martin, S.J.
Author of *Jesus: A Pilgrimage*

"Fr. Reed's exceedingly valuable book is filled with compelling insights and inspirations that can and will enliven the faith of all!"

Msgr. Joseph G. Quinn
Vice President, University Mission and Ministry
Ford University

"This gentle guide to growth in faith teaches through saints, scripture, and people in our own lives. Fr. Reed provides an easy-to-use tool for individuals and groups who seek to deepen their awareness of God."

Sr. Mary Ann Walsh, R.S.M.
Director of Media Relations
US Conference of Catholic Bishops

"One of the modern Church's great communicators is communicating something great with this book. Fr. Robert Reed has given us an inspiring look at how saints have transformed our world—and how they can transform each of us. Take, read, share. You will be (as the title so aptly puts it) renewed!"

Deacon Greg Kandra
Blogger at *The Deacon's Bench*

D0424282

"Pope Francis proclaims the joy of the Gospel. Be joyful and share the Good News. Fr. Reed's book offers practical, hopeful, and insightful ways to do so. An inspiring read."

Sr. Marian Batho, C.S.J.
Delegate for Religious
Archdiocese of Boston

"If you've ever sat in the pew and pondered how you could share your passion for the Good News of the Gospel, then *Renewed* will serve both as your inspirational marching orders and the primer you need to become a part of the New Evangelization. Both practical and reflective, this resource is perfect for individual or group contemplation and gives each of us the tools needed to bring the treasures of the Church to a world in great need of its gifts."

Lisa M. Hendey
Author of *The Grace of Yes*

"If, like me, you've ever struggled to incorporate devotions to saints into your daily prayer life, allow Fr. Reed to introduce you to these spiritual guides who want to bring you closer to Jesus than ever before. The first chapter alone hit me right between the eyes."

Greg Willits
Author of *The New Evangelization and You*

RENEWED

Ten Ways

to

Rediscover the Saints,

Embrace Your Gifts,

and

Revive

Your Catholic Faith

Robert P. Reed

ave maria press AMP notre dame, indiana

Founded in 1865, Ave Maria Press is a ministry of the United States Province of Holy Cross.

www.avemariapress.com

Paperback: ISBN-13 978-1-59471-470-2

E-book: ISBN-13 978-1-59471-471-9

Cover images of Sts. John Paul II, Augustine, Edith Stein, Joan of Arc, Thérèse of Lisieux, and Thomas Aquinas © 2014 by Tracy L. Christianson, TLC Portraits, www.portraitsofsaints.com.

Cover design by Brian C. Conley.

Text design by Katherine Robinson.

Printed and bound in the United States of America.

Library of Congress Cataloging-in-Publication Data

CONTENTS

FOREWORD

While there is widespread support among Catholics today for the idea of the New Evangelization, many wonder: What can I do? Where should I start? In this clarion call to renewal, Father Robert Reed challenges all of us—laity, religious, deacons, priests, and bishops—to start by looking within and making an honest assessment of our gifts and the ways we can better put them to use to revitalize the Church.

Father Reed rightly highlights one of the greatest resources available to us: the example and intercession of the saints. Rather than simply selecting a single saint to imitate, he instead proposes pairs of saints who at first glance seem like unlikely companions, like Augustine and Joan of Arc or Athanasius and Mother Teresa. By juxtaposing two saints he finds new perspectives. From Aquinas and Therese we learn that we need both the mind and the heart. From Paul and John Vianney we come to appreciate that the Gospel is best proclaimed through relationships. From Isidore and Fulton Sheen we see the courage at work to use new technologies. Like Catholics today, these saints lived in times of crises, but through God's grace and their creative energy, they found a way forward. With their help, we can too!

Father Reed's down-to-earth and encouraging lessons are both persuasive and practical. He suggests ten steps we can all take, and he provides prayers, scripture readings, application steps, and reflection questions that are just right for any parish group and for personal reflection. Father Reed is already well known for his parish ministry and his work on The CatholicTV Network, an apostolate of the Archdiocese of Boston and America's Catholic Television Network. This book is yet another helpful contribution toward enlivening the Church and will, I hope, reach an even greater audience throughout the Church.

Cardinal Seán O'Malley, O.F.M. Cap.
Archbishop of Boston

PREFACE

It was the fall of 1965, just before the close of the Second Vatican Council. I was sitting at my desk in classroom 1A at St. John the Evangelist School in Swampscott, Massachusetts. It took Sister Lydia, C.S.J., probably ninety seconds to tell us the story of Saint Tarcisius. She was doing her job; she was fulfilling her vocation. It was a moment in time. But I have never forgotten that moment, that story, and the nun who told it.

During the third century, she recounted, Christians had to meet secretly in the catacombs to avoid persecution. A boy named Tarcisius (I imagined him to be my age) volunteered to take the Holy Eucharist to Christians in prison. On his way there, he encountered a group of friends who invited him to play with them. Knowing that he was a Christian and curious about what is was that he was carrying in the fold of his garment, the gang of boys tried to pry it out of his grasp. Eventually the group of boys evolved into an angry mob that overcame Tarcisius, mortally injuring him. He died as he was being carried back to the catacombs, the Eucharist still held to his chest.

In listening with rapt attention to that simple story, this little boy sitting near the back of a first-grade classroom learned that belief in Jesus' true presence in the Eucharist goes back to the earliest and most challenging days of Christianity and that the very Body and Blood of the Lord has always been worth defending. I also discovered that God does not reserve heroism for adults. Children, too, are capable of loving Jesus so much that they would be willing to die for him. In that moment, my

understanding of myself as a Christian was confirmed
and the seed of a vocation to the ordained priesthood
was planted.

Thank you, Sr. Lydia, and thanks to the Sisters of
St. Joseph of Boston. Since I first learned of the witness
of Tarcisius, I have prayed for the courage to willingly
give my life for Christ, even though I am the world's biggest chicken. But I knew that God would give me what
I needed. What I needed most were companions on the
journey. All along the way, God has provided them for
me. I have observed, studied, and known many inspiring
people. We never walk alone when we allow God to use
us for his glory. I am grateful for all of them.

In the cathedral church of the Archdiocese of Los
Angeles dedicated to Our Lady of the Angels, an origi-
nally unplanned display of tapestries demonstrates the
need for companions with visual conviction. The work
represents great disciples, some young and some old,
interspersed with people like you and me, all streaming
toward the sanctuary and the Holy Sacrifice. To stand in
that center aisle and look around provides a profound
catechesis on the giftedness of the Church now and
through the centuries.

This book is intended for anyone who asks: "What
can we do; where do we go from here; how do we find
the courage?" Certainly the Church, built upon the rock
of Peter's confession of faith, will prevail. The Church is
Christ, and Christ has been raised. But since we are all
members of his Body, there must be a constant reckoning.
We can recount the crises that the Church has faced in
the past until we are blue in the face. But, unless we face
the present crisis with a personal praxis and corporate
strategy that is up to the challenge, we are full of hot air.

The insights of this book are not fully my own, but represent lessons learned by observation and collaboration. With great excitement Saint Paul wrote to the Ephesians that we have been redeemed and God has been immeasurably generous toward us (Eph 1:3–10). If God has indeed given us the wisdom to understand fully the mysteries, the plan he was pleased to decree in Christ, then we need to reach deeply within ourselves, joining our minds and hands together with humility and courage. God has made possible the fitness of the Catholic faith for every age.

For the sake of the world, the challenge is to rediscover and renew our gifts. This project cannot wait.

INTRODUCTION

Renewing the face of the earth began long ago. Some see the renewal as beginning at the nativity of Jesus of Nazareth. Some count its days from the call of Abraham by a God his forebears did not know. And some say it began at the very beginning, not east of Eden but within that primordial garden where the Hebrew scriptures place the origins of humanity.

Wherever and whenever you might believe it began, God initiated the project of renewing the earth to be in relationship with the human family, to call people into community with the Divine and with one another, and to save humanity by that love without limits made incarnate in the Son of God, Jesus Christ. Since the decades following Jesus' death on the Cross and the proclamation of his resurrection, this project has generally been called "the Church." Rooted in the Hebrew *qahal yhwh* and the Greek *ekklesia*, the Church is the gathering of God's people, the assembly of God. In the Church God calls us together in his sight and in his saving love.

But though the initiative is divine, the response is human. Each of us must respond to God's call into his saving community. God calls us to accept and carry on the mission Jesus has handed on to us. Every generation has borne this responsibility. And, in our generation, we too are responsible for the Church's health and vitality, for her ability to respond to the opportunities presented by these times, and for her capacity to overcome the obstacles of new circumstances. The Gospel remains and endures in its original form, but the eyes and ears and minds of those who are to receive the good news must do it within the culture of this time, perhaps despite the culture of this time. To be heard, the Gospel must be authentic and spoken in the language of those who might listen. To minister effectively and to celebrate in a way that others will experience as celebration, we must respond anew in our age to God's unchanging love.

This response, this renewal, this adaptation, this faithful passing on of the Gospel by whatever means necessary: this is the Holy Spirit's project to renew the face of the earth.

To be successful in its execution, any idea, program, or project requires innovation to survive and prosper. Innovation becomes part of the labor of any working concept, even if the idea has already taken the form of an institution. In fact, innovation becomes perhaps even more important within the institution so that the idea maintains its liveliness and appeal. Throughout time, this has been the story of the institution we know as the Catholic Church. Its members, ordinary people who have received the Gospel into their hearts, have, by the grace of God, responded with imagination to the responsibility to live and teach the good news to their own generation. In every generation to lesser or greater extent, the Church has had to renew itself to be effective in the new era in which it finds itself.

On occasion, however, a generation is called to undertake this creative innovation in a period of greater-than-usual tumult. The period following the invention of the printing press was such a time, as communication to the masses became exponentially easier and fundamental questions were raised as to what this spread of knowledge, including the wide availability of the Bible, would portend. Such revolutionary times, as opposed to the more ordinary evolutionary periods of gradual change, ask more of the Church and of her clergy and laity. Much more. There have been times of crisis in the development of the Church, times in which momentous decisions must be made.

It has become trite to speak of a *crisis* as both a moment of danger and of opportunity. But some truisms, however trite, are still true. This moment in the development of the Church is one of dangerous opportunity. There is a venerable Chinese curse, "May you live in an interesting time." We certainly do. You and I live in a time of danger, opportunity, and interest: ours is a moment that invites us to transmute curse into blessing.

Derived from the verb *krino*, meaning to separate, distinguish, or judge, the Greek term κρίσις (*krisis*) means "decision" or "judgment". Its likely first meaning denotes divine judgment, a decision coming down from God. But its secondary meaning calls for judgment on our part, on the human side. A time of crisis, then, is a time to judge what may be done, to make a decision to do something, and then to do it.

Our own time is a point of crisis for both the Church and the society within which she lives, breathes, preaches, and celebrates. What does this crisis require of us? Our answer to this serious question will determine nothing less than the credibility of the Gospel of Jesus Christ for this generation and the next. What we do will determine nothing less than the vitality of the Church in the first century of the third Christian millennium.

More than a decade into his twenty-seven-year pontificate, Pope John Paul II issued a call for a "new evangelization." By this he indicated a renewed and newly effective announcement of the message of Jesus Christ to persons and populations who had already historically both heard and received that message. It was a call to renewal. Response to this call has been broad and various, including new institutes, collaborations, media, books, and blogs. I recently googled "new evangelization" and 914,000 results appeared in 0.23 seconds (surely there will be more results by the time you read these words). We have a million newspaper, magazine, and encyclopedia articles on the subject. There are organizations and offices dedicated to the New Evangelization, including those privately founded, those run by dioceses, and those established by the Holy See in Rome. There are many reports from synods on the topic, with commentary on those reports which are followed by reports on the commentaries.

Within the pontificate of Benedict XVI the effort for a new evangelization continued. Pope Benedict established the Pontifical Council for Promoting the New Evangelization and devoted a meeting of the synod of bishops to the "New Evangelization for the Transmission of the Christian Faith." For more than two decades now, *new evangelization* has been the byword for the revitalization of the mission of the Church.

But this revitalization must begin with and in you. It can only flow from the deep interior joy of discipleship. In his Apostolic Exhortation *Evangelii Gaudium* (The Joy of the Gospel), Pope Francis calls us to create a culture of encounter by first revisiting and revitalizing our own friendship with Jesus, the author and finisher of our faith. If our interior life is caught up in itself (and how tempting this is) and not in the quiet, deep joy that comes in drawing close to the heart of the risen Christ, the impetus for a new evangelization will be wanting in us.

I invite all Christians, everywhere, at this very moment, to a renewed personal encounter with Jesus Christ, or at least an openness to letting him encounter them; I ask all of you to do this unfailingly each day .... May nothing inspire more than his life, which impels us onward!

The book in your hands can be read within that context of the New Evangelization, for it comes at this crucial point in Church history. But, in another sense, the project this book sets forth is prior to the New Evangelization. This book is a primer, a precursor to the great work of the New Evangelization. My aim is to provide a starting point for renewing the giftedness of the Church, to spur the innovation of a dynamic of ecclesial life consistent with a twenty-first-century mindset and predisposed for an evangelization that works.

Or, to put it another way, I want to raise this question: how would a Church look, sound, and act if it is to be effective in renewing Christian faith in the world? What does the Church need to do to reach the young urban professional on the east side of Manhattan, the dispirited grandmother in suburban Birmingham, England, and the mother trying to keep herself and her children alive in sub-Saharan Africa? What does the Church need to do to earn a new hearing from gay people, atheists, and the many men and women of all ages who, for many different reasons, have given up hope in the words and person of Jesus Christ? Can you picture what the Church needs to become? Can you hear what it needs to say? That attempt to picture and to hear is what we are about here.

Each chapter in this book provides a distinct call to which we must respond if we are to be collaborators with the Holy Spirit in the renewal of the Church that is needed today. These are steps that we can all take, regardless of our place in the Church. Whether we are ordained, religious, or laity, we all have an essential part to play. To help us respond with imagination, there are a number of practical aids at the end of each chapter. Most importantly, there is a call to prayer and reflection on scripture. A biblical passage is provided for *lectio divina,* or sacred reading. In his Angelus address on November 6, 2005, Pope Benedict described lectio divina this way:

> It consists in pouring over a biblical text for some time, reading it and rereading it, as it were, "ruminating" on it as the Fathers say and squeezing from it, so to speak, all its "juice," so that it may nourish meditation and contemplation and, like water, succeed in irrigating life itself.

The chapters also contain suggestions for application. Because change begins individually, they ask us first to look within and make personal changes so that we can then be more effective agents of renewal in our local situations. The chapters also contain questions for reflection and sharing, perhaps in a small group. When we gather together, we discover the Spirit of Christ at work within each of us and among us.

To be the Church is to be in community. It is blessedly true, as the Letter to the Hebrews proclaims at the opening of its twelfth chapter, that we are surrounded by a "great a cloud of witnesses," those who have gone before us in the faith. This work reflects on the lives of some heroes of Christian discipleship through the centuries. These saints are examples to us of men and women who, living in their own times, whether times of ordinary or extraordinary change, made incarnate the Gospel of Jesus Christ in their own choices and in so doing built the Church. They allowed God's call to assemble as his people to be heard with clarity, simplicity, and joy. This was their project in the sight of God. They did it. And so will we, if we choose to incarnate the Gospel of Jesus Christ in our own time.

1.

DISCOVER AND RECEIVE YOUR GIFTS

Thomas Aquinas and Thérèse of Lisieux

In our times the Church is under attack from within and from without. It is buffeted by scandal, hindered by lack of clergy, and stressed by a long period of change we cannot control or sometimes even follow. We look around and say, "What has happened to the Church? Where are the strength, vision, and purpose I used to enjoy? Does the Church have a future?"

In light of our daily experience and the headlines, these questions seem reasonable. We have been living all our lives in a time of social revolution. The changes challenge us to adapt as individuals. The Church must do the same—find a way to adapt to this rapidly evolving culture of materialism, secularism, pleasure-seeking, and technology. As individuals and as a Christian community, we need to keep our balance and find a way to glorify God in serving others. The world may not know it, but we know that it is starving to experience the love

of God. That is our perennial mission in every generation, to reveal Jesus, Lord and Savior.

There are very legitimate reasons for discouragement all around us. Consider these:

- Most of our parish churches see many fewer families
  on Sundays to celebrate the Eucharist.

- National studies show that our young people cannot
  articulate the faith they profess to hold, and many of
  their elders cannot either.

- The Church is diminishing in the northern hemi-
  sphere, though thankfully growing in the southern.
  What does this shift mean now and in the future for
  the identity of the Church?

- We seem divided between those who listen atten-
  tively to the voices of Church leadership in the nation
  and from Rome, and those who find little sustenance
  in those voices for their faith.

Yet ours is not the first generation to face massive
challenges in the life of the Catholic Church. The story
of the Church is a dark tapestry of obstacles, heresies,
excesses, deprivations, persecutions, plagues, and blood-
shed. We have gazed into the gates of hell, but they could
not prevail against us. The Church marches on just as
Jesus promised, and we have his word that it will endure
for all time and eternity—for it is his Church, not ours.

Where Do We Start?

If as Christians we want to bear fruit in our service to
others, we need grace. There are many needs inside and
outside the Church. Where do we start? There is, in fact,
only one starting point: the Holy Spirit.

The apostle Paul often spoke about grace in his letters to the first Christian communities. He urged people to be aware of the gifts that God was pouring out into their midst. These gifts included believing, understanding, preaching, healing, and loving. In his first letter to the Corinthians, we read:

> To each is given the manifestation of the Spirit for the common good. To one is given through the Spirit the utterance of wisdom, and to another the utterance of knowledge according to the same Spirit, to another faith by the same Spirit, to another gifts of healing by the one Spirit, to another the working of miracles, to another prophecy, to another the discernment of spirits, to another various kinds of tongues, to another the interpretation of tongues. All these are activated by one and the same Spirit, who allots to each one individually just as the Spirit chooses. (1 Cor 12:7–11)

For Saint Paul, it's all about the Holy Spirit. In three sentences he refers to the Holy Spirit seven times. The Holy Spirit is the origin of all the gifts, talents, and abilities we need to be of service to others. We have natural abilities too, of course, which are also gifts from God, but even those natural abilities need to be transformed by the Spirit, or grace, if we want to bear fruit, if we want to serve others as Jesus did.

Paul points us to another essential gift as well: the gift of freedom in Jesus Christ. Through Christ we now have freedom from sin and death, and freedom to live for others. So the apostle urges believers in Galatia to grasp and retain that gift: "For freedom Christ has set us free. Stand firm, therefore, and do not submit again to a yoke of slavery" (Gal 5:1). Paul was urging those to whom he carried the Gospel to recognize that they were immersed in a world of grace, in an unending sea of divine gifts.

Early Christians were equipped for service by grace. But like us they must have found it difficult at times to recognize their gifts. In many pastoral letters, Saint Paul had to exhort them strongly to stir up the grace of God within them. Too often they complained about problems, found faults in one another, formed factions, and even resisted the apostle who taught them. Saint Paul's most important correction to these first believers was to remind them that God in Jesus Christ was indeed with them, loving them, and daily giving them all that they needed to grow and serve. "All things are yours," he wrote, "whether Paul or Apollos or Cephas or the world or life or death or the present or the future—all belong to you, and you belong to Christ, and Christ belongs to God" (1 Cor 3:21–23).

Remember when God fed the Israelites manna in the wilderness?

> When the layer of dew lifted, there on the surface of the wilderness was a fine flaky substance, as fine as frost on the ground. When the Israelites saw it, they said to one another, "What is it?" For they did not know what it was. Moses said to them, "It is the bread that the LORD has given you to eat." (Ex 16:13–15)

The gift of bread was constantly given from above, until the people were able to raise their own food in that land which was itself a gift.

Like the Israelites, we may not recognize God's gifts to us. Or we might think they are inadequate to the needs at hand. But notice that the manna given to the Israelites each day was sufficient to feed them that day. They received enough for one day only, and they had to learn that they would receive it each morning without fail. It was God's wise way of teaching them to trust him, to rely on God's daily bread even in the dire circumstances of wandering for years in the desert.

To live open to God is to live receiving God's gifts, be it desert bread, wisdom to teach, or freedom to live the faith. But so often we do not recognize God's gifts to us, or we fear that those gifts are inadequate to the need, or we wonder and worry that those gifts will cease. That's how it was with the communities Saint Paul knew. That's how it was with the nation Moses was leading in God's sight. And that's how it is with us.

We humans are funny. We are more likely to fuss and fret about what we don't have (or seem to have) than to thank God for what we do have. Human nature is the same, but, thankfully, so is God. In the beginning he set a garden on the surface of the earth as the perfect place for man and woman to live. God is still providing what we need, both in times of plenty and in times of want. God knows what we need, even if it isn't always what we desire. The lesson of scripture is that what we need is what is given to us. God is trustworthy to give without ceasing as long as the need is there. God's faithfulness is based squarely upon the truth of the shortest definition of God offered in the Christian scriptures—perhaps anywhere: "God is love" (1 Jn 4:8). And love's nature is to give of itself to others. God gives to us continuously, generously. We need only to receive the gifts and begin to enjoy them to use them.

We are grateful that those who met the tests of their own times serve as examples and encouragement in ours. They help us know that we too belong to a gifted

Church with proven staying power and the ability to adjust in healthy fashion to baffling new circumstances.

A man and a woman, each born into Christ's family in the month of January almost 650 years apart, have much to teach us about our own giftedness. They show us the way to use our gifts for our own good, the good of others, the good of the Church, and the ultimate glory of God.

Thomas Aquinas

Thomas Aquinas was a man of the thirteenth century. His was a century of Crusades that ended with the Christian Jerusalem kingdom falling under the authority of the Sultan of Egypt. Meanwhile wars engulfed Europe from England to Russia. There were repeated hostilities between the papacy and the Holy Roman Empire. It was a time in which even the oldest universities in Europe were still relatively young and vulnerable. The scholastic method was still largely undeveloped.

Yet in the midst of this tumult and uncertainty, this was an age of renewal in the Church. New institutions sprang up to replace what had grown old, ineffective, and frail. In 1209 the Order of Friars Minor, founded by Francis of Assisi, was approved by the papacy. Just seven years later the Order of Preachers, founded by Dominic, received its own endorsement. Less than a decade later Thomas Aquinas was born. As a young man, he joined the Order of Preachers over the objections of his family. He was destined, along with Bonaventure, to become one of the greatest Dominicans—indeed, one of the most influential thinkers the world has known.

Over a brief lifetime, moving around Europe at the behest of his Dominican superiors, Aquinas sought a deeper understanding of the faith. Under his hand, the Scholastic method developed, giving impetus to thought and progress within the Church and society. Aquinas considered the nature of God and the worth and the purpose of human life. He engaged in the theological controversies of his time, effectively exposing error where he found it. At the same time in his writings, he created a positive and comprehensive exposition of the Christian faith.

Let's explore the method of Aquinas to see if it may contain an insight for us. In his *Summa Theologica*, as well as in many of his other works, Aquinas used teaching from those who had thought and written before him, whether they were Christians or not. He often cited Saint Augustine, one of the Doctors of the Church, but he also cited Aristotle, whom he often referred to as "the Philosopher"; Averroes, the Islamic scholar (Ibn Rušd); and Moses ben Maimon (Maimonides), the Jewish philosopher and scholar of the Torah. The latter two had lived in the decades of the century just prior to Aquinas's own. Thomas was certain of the unity of truth flowing from the one source, the one God, and so he was unafraid to seek and speak the truth wherever he found it. He was armed with the belief that all truth is God's truth.

Thomas Aquinas drank deeply from all the wells of learning he had available to him: scripture, Church tradition, mystics, classical philosophers, and the wisdom of other traditions. From these he wove a brilliant explanation of Christian faith which included an invitation to know God. In his work he gave us a way of understanding human living that has endured into our own time and will continue to illuminate thought in the ages ahead.

And yet, despite all of his great contributions, toward the end of his life Aquinas ceased his work. He told his faithful secretary that all he had written seemed to him "like so much straw." Catholic tradition holds that an aging Thomas on one occasion had a vision of Christ who asked him what it was he desired in return for all he had done. Thomas replied, "Only You, Lord." All his understanding of God and his attributes, and all his writings, seemed to him like so much straw compared to the treasure and glory of the risen Lord. In saying "Only You, Lord" he reveals to us the motive at the heart of who he was and what he did. The desire for God, which may have seemed like a lack in his life, became the driving force that enabled Aquinas to serve believers and the entire Church for centuries to come.

THÉRÈSE OF LISIEUX

The Carmelite nun, Saint Thérèse of Lisieux, often called the Little Flower, was born into the same faith centuries after the death of Thomas Aquinas. She was raised in a devoutly religious family. Both of her parents had desired themselves to enter religious life. Thérèse and her two older sisters answered the call to religious life. In her spiritual autobiography, *Story of a Soul*, Thérèse describes her first longing to love and serve Jesus even before she could express her desire in speech.

When she was fifteen, with the support of her father, Thérèse pressed her case to the prioress of the Carmel of Lisieux to enter the monastery despite her young age. When she was refused, she persisted in her suit to the diocesan bishop and finally to the pope himself. While traveling with a diocesan pilgrimage, Thérèse found herself at an audience of Pope Leo XIII. Everyone was permitted to kneel before the Holy Father, kiss his ring, and receive his blessing, but they were instructed not to speak to his holiness. When her turn came, however, Thérèse spoke. She told the pope her vocation story in a few heartfelt words, and she asked him to help her enter Carmel.

Though the pope did not intervene in her case, the young woman's boldness and determination made an impression upon all. She was soon received into Carmel. As she began her life there, she had only nine more years to live. She spent them in prayer, in service to her sisters, and in a profound deepening of her spiritual life.

Thanks to a request from her prioress, Sister Agnes of Jesus, who also happened to be Thérèse's birth sister Pauline, we have a book that reveals what occurred in the soul of Thérèse at various stages in her brief life. *Story of a Soul* and her letters to her family reveal the Spirit of God at work. Her inner life was one of passionate devotion to the Savior. She was joined to Jesus by the bond of love.

Yet, like so many of the saints who have experienced the depths of God, her spiritual life was not one continuous victory and joy. She came to recognize over time that her strong personality needed to be submerged and perfected. This work took place in the day-to-day life at Carmel through ordinary contact with her sisters there. Sister Thérèse sought out those members of the community to whom she was least attracted humanly. She served them, sought to understand them, and excused their apparent deficiencies as covering over deeper gifts of faith and love. Her account of these years is an extraordinary witness to finding holiness in our most mundane circumstances, for often it is in our closest relationships that we cultivate superiorities, resentments, and coldness.

In her relationship to the Divine, Thérèse knew long periods of spiritual dryness in which nothing felt real to her. In chapter 9 of her spiritual memoir, she finds words to describe this time:

> But during the Paschal days, so full of light, our Lord made me understand that there really are in truth souls bereft of Faith and Hope, who, through abuse of grace, lose these precious treasures, the only source of pure and lasting joy. He allowed my soul to be overwhelmed with darkness, and the thought of Heaven, which had consoled me from my earliest childhood, now became a subject of conflict and torture. This trial did not last merely for days or weeks; I have been suffering for months, and I still await deliverance.[1]

Thérèse suffered severely through this experience, but even within it she came to see that she could offer that suffering for the good of others. And she had confidence that her bond to the Lord was secure.

> But, dear Lord, Thy child has understood Thou art the Light Divine; she asks Thy pardon for her unbelieving brethren, and is willing to eat the bread of sorrow as long as Thou mayest wish. For love of Thee she will sit at that table of bitterness where these poor sinners take their food, and she will not stir from it until Thou givest the sign. But may she not say in her own name, and the name of her guilty brethren: "O God, be merciful to us sinners!" Send us away justified.[2]

The high point of her lifelong effort to recognize, embrace, and express her own vocation came in the insight she shares in the eleventh chapter of *Story of a Soul*. Sister Thérèse writes with great energy of the desire she felt to be a priest, crusader, prophet, apostle, teacher of the faith, missionary, and martyr. Allowing the apostle Paul's first letter to the Corinthians to be her guide, she strives to find her own place in the Church:

> Considering the mystical body of the Church, I had not recognized myself in any of the members described by Saint Paul, or rather I desired to see myself in them all. Charity gave me the key to my vocation. I understood that if the Church had a body composed of different members, the most necessary and most noble of all could not be lacking to it, and so I understood that the Church had a Heart and that this Heart was *burning with love.* I understood it was Love alone that made the Church's members act, that if *Love ever became extinct, apostles would not preach the Gospel and martyrs would not shed their blood. I understood that Love comprised all vocations, that Love was everything, that it embraced all times and places . . . in a word, that it was eternal!*
>
> Then, in the excess of my delirious joy, I cried out: O Jesus, my Love . . . my vocation, at last I have found it. . . . *my vocation is Love!*
>
> Yes, I have found my place in the Church and it is you, O my God, who have given me this place; in the heart of the Church, my mother, I shall be *Love.*[3]

This vocation was not only to be hers while she still lived here on earth. Thérèse's vocation found its truest and fullest expression after death, in the presence of God, in the company of Jesus. She now lives within the reality of Saint Paul's words:

> Love never ends. . . . For now we see in a mirror, dimly, but then we will see face to face. Now I know

> only in part; then I will know fully, even as I have
> been fully known. And now faith, hope, and love
> abide, these three; and the greatest of these is love.
> (1 Cor 13:8, 12–13)

Sister Thérèse would continue to be love, and to attract others to love God with the same faithfulness, intensity, and joy as she had done, and still does. This beloved saint is a Doctor of the Church, the patroness of missionaries, and the friend of countless souls who continue to come to her for intercession. Thomas and Thérèse are siblings to one another, and to us. What joins them is not a "what" but a "who," the person of Jesus Christ.

WHAT THOMAS AQUINAS AND THÉRÈSE OF LISIEUX CAN TEACH US

At first glance Thomas Aquinas seems to have given his mind over to the service of Christ and Thérèse of Lisieux her heart to the same Lord. But to focus on this contrast of gifts is to miss what is most important in each of them, and the most important thing they have to teach us.

Yes, Thomas Aquinas possessed an amazing intellect, an open spirit, an indefatigable energy. But we diminish if we fail to see that Aquinas gave not just his mind, but his whole self to God, and he placed his whole self at God's service. Giving all to God is the key to everything Aquinas did and was. His work illustrates that he wanted the same for everyone. He wanted everyone to know Jesus Christ, the Jesus he met in the scriptures and the Christ he found in Church tradition. More than just his mind, Thomas Aquinas gave his heart and soul and his whole being to the Lord Jesus. By abiding in Jesus, Thomas contributed much to the life and work of the Church.

And it is true that Thérèse Martin, the girl of Lisieux, had a heart made for great love. From her earliest years, her deep and sensitive love bonded her to her family, but it also sometimes challenged them with its intensity. Drawn to the Carmelite life because it would call her to be joined to the Lord Jesus with a lasting and unbreakable love, her way of loving was deepened and purified by experience. But we sell her short if we think that Sister Thérèse was made of mere emotion. Her intellect, her will, and her every energy of body, soul, and spirit were engaged in the work, the fatiguing labor of learning how to love.

Again, Aquinas was not a disembodied mind, and the young Carmelite of Lisieux was not a capricious, rapturous heart. The medieval theologian reasoned in a manner that included the heart. The sister in Carmel sought love with a firm and disciplined mindfulness. Separated by hundreds of miles, hundreds of years, by changes of culture and language, they were both Catholic. They were both committed to the faith and to expressing it in its noblest form to those around them. Both discovered and employed their God-given gifts.

We live in the same Church of grace in which they believed and sought and thought. We have received the gifts that they received. In fact, we have more than they had because we have them, their thoughts, prayers, and examples, to lead us forward. We have what Saint Thomas and Saint Thérèse won by effort and faithfulness. We are their successors. We too live among the gifts of the Holy Spirit in a remarkable age. We too are called to the dedication and devotion that receives and acts upon the gifts that God has already given to us.

Next Steps

Prayer to the Holy Spirit for Gifts

True God, you were there at the creation of the world. By your breath you gave life to men and women, and you placed the earth under our care. Breathe on us again, Lord, and reveal to us our natural gifts. After Jesus ascended to the Father, you fell upon his humble followers and gave them power to bear the Gospel into all the world. Fall on us again, Lord, and reveal to us our spiritual gifts. We gratefully receive all your gifts and place them in your service. We seek you, Holy Spirit, that we may serve the needs of others with love and do the work of your Church with power, that all may give you glory forever. Amen.

Lectio Divina

I am the vine, you are the branches. Those who abide in me and I in them bear much fruit, because apart from me you can do nothing. (Jn 15:5)

✳✳✳

One day Peter and John were going up to the temple at the hour of prayer, at three o'clock in the afternoon. And a man lame from birth was being carried in. People would lay him daily at the gate of the temple called the Beautiful Gate so that he could ask for alms from those entering the temple. When he saw Peter and John about to go into the temple, he asked them for alms. Peter looked intently at him, as did John, and said, "Look at us." And he fixed his attention on them, expecting to receive something from them. But Peter said, "I have no silver or gold, but what I have I give you; in the name of Jesus Christ of Nazareth, stand up and walk." And he took him by the right hand and raised him up; and immediately his feet and ankles were made strong. Jumping up, he stood and began to walk, and he entered the temple with them, walking and leaping and praising God. (Acts 3:1–8)

Application

To participate in renewing the gifts of the Church, it is most important that you engage in reflection. Focus your reflection today on discovering and receiving your gifts. Your personal reflection on your gifts may include reflection on the gifts that you receive within your parish, campus, or other organization involved in ministry to the Church or to the world. The following steps may help you in this process:

1. Seeking clarity of heart and soul, confess your failures.

2. Recount your successes, especially those you have found deeply satisfying.

3. Consider what you most admire about a favorite or patron saint.

4. Inventory your gifts: physical, mental, emotional, social, and spiritual.

Questions

1. Do you lead with your head, like Thomas Aquinas, or with your heart, like Thérèse?

2. Do you, like Thérèse, feel uncertain about your vocation? Your gifts?

3. Can you say with Aquinas, "Only You, Lord"?

4. If you could have any *natural* gift you wanted, what would it be?

5. If you could have any *spiritual* gift you wanted, what would it be?

6. What is your greatest concern for others?

7. What is your greatest concern for the Church today?

8. What one thing would you most like to accomplish this year? This decade?

9. Are you willing to ask God for the gifts you need to accomplish that goal?

Notes

1. Thérèse of Lisieux, *Story of a Soul* (New York: Cosimo Publications, 1997), 124.

2. Ibid., 124–125.

3. Thérèse of Lisieux, *Story of a Soul* (Washington, DC: ICS Publications, 1996), 194.

2.

LOOK BEYOND THE PRESENT TROUBLES

Augustine of Hippo and Joan of Arc

We can easily feel bad as we look out at the present state of the Church and society. We might ask ourselves: Who ever lived in a world like this one? Who knows where things are going from here? And who is actually finding meaning and a better quality of life through the Church? Fewer and fewer Americans are involved with their churches, and this is true across denominations. After a century of stability, even the percentage of Americans who say they believe in God has begun to drop. Meanwhile, we see a growing number of those who believe the human family would be better off if there were no religions.

Recent studies like the US Religious Landscape Survey by the Pew Forum on Religion and Public Life reveal that *former* Roman Catholics now make up one of the largest religious groups in the country. These are Catholics who have moved to other denominations or to no faith practice at all. They have their reasons, some better

than others, but we are left with the fact that the Church
Jesus Christ founded upon the rock of Peter seems to be
in serious decline in our country and in our own time.
How many of us are optimistic about the future of our
secular society? Can we help but feel pessimistic about
the Church of tomorrow?

The prospects for the US Church in our generation
and the next can seem dim, grim, and dire. But that's
just one way of looking at it. Widening the lens through
which we see our present situation can help. By consid-
ering today's problems and challenges in the light of our
past, we may discover some surprising things. We may
be surprised by hope. The problems and challenges our
forebears faced and overcame long ago may reveal our
present situation for what it is: grave, but not lost. We
are not at the point of Armageddon, as some believe.
Let's look to Augustine of Hippo and Joan of Arc for
inspiration and strategies to help us renew the Church
in our own time.

Augustine of Hippo

During the summer of 430 AD, Augustine lay dying in
the city and diocese he had long served as bishop, Hippo
Regius. This giant of the Church spent his last days
watching and praying from his deathbed as the tribe
known as the Vandals besieged his city. He felt helpless.
Ultimately the invaders conquered Hippo Regius and
made it the capital of their kingdom in North Africa.
Augustine, who had spent his adult life since his conversion to Christianity defending and explaining the faith,
could now only watch as his city fell prey to a tribe who
had converted to Arianism, a heretical view of Christ
that he had spent much time and energy opposing for

decades. Augustine was experiencing the beginning of the end of the vital, creative, and energized Christian presence in North Africa.

Two decades earlier, as another tribe, the Visigoths, attacked and overcame Rome itself, Augustine had taken up his pen to write *City of God*. In that masterpiece of theology, he defended Christianity from the fear-filled response by many at that time to the sacking of Rome. Many argued that Rome's conversion to Christianity from its ancient Roman religions had doomed the city, and ultimately the Roman Empire. In response, Augustine wrote of the existence of two cities, the City of Man and the City of God.

> The City of God we speak of is the same to which testimony is borne by that Scripture, which excels all the writings of the nations by its divine authority. . . . There is a city of God, and its Founder has inspired us with love which makes us covet its citizenship. To this Founder of the holy city the citizens of the earthly city prefer their own gods.[1]

Augustine drew out the nature of the two cities, differentiating them from one another chiefly by the love that energizes each. "Two cities have been formed by two loves: the earthly by the love of self, even to the contempt of God; the heavenly by the love of God, even to the contempt of self."[2] One looks for glory for self here and now. The other seeks only God's glory.

Across the depth and breadth of human effort, Augustine reveals the work of and for God. He affirms God's presence. He foresees the ultimate victory of God's will for creation, for humanity, and for history. What endures in the end, what brings fulfillment, order, and peace at last is the inevitable revelation of the City of God.

Somehow, in the midst of a time of unparalleled chaos and terror, this man of intelligence and faith managed to take the broadest possible view of the meaning of the moment. No one then living, nor any who had lived in ages past, had ever experienced the times in which people had now found themselves. He chose to receive and share the gift of God's perspective in this massive text. Seen from the perspective of God's ultimate plan for the world and for humanity, even the fall of the capital city of the empire, as devastating as that event was, was only a single moment in a history of great length and complexity, with a future stretching before that moment of unknowable length and unimaginable complexity, even like the complexity of our own times. Saint Augustine seized his present moment and held it close to God with the assurance that humanity and the Church would go on. The earthly city and the heavenly city would continue, sometimes uneasily, to coexist until the end of time.

So, now, two decades later, the great thinker lay on his deathbed, his own city of Hippo in flames and chaos, like that which Rome had experienced earlier. Just as he had experienced the fall of Rome with trust in God, we must surmise that Bishop Augustine looked at the conflagration around him with a calm confidence in the father of Jesus Christ. He trusted in Christ in a time of terror, and everything around him was falling to pieces. He trusted that the Creator of the heavenly city would maintain its foundations and ensure its continued life and growth.

There is a temptation to romanticize moments like this one, to be over-zealous in trying to show the holiness or greatness of a saint. But the truth always serves God better than even the most well-intentioned exaggerations. The facts are clear: Augustine and his people experienced horrible destruction in their time, yet Augustine died in faith, believing that a loving God is in charge, despite all that his eyes and ears were telling him at the end. Though singular, even rare, Augustine's faith was not unreasonable. It is a great virtue to look beyond present troubles to future success. In the midst of anarchy and unholy disorder, Augustine could see God's own peace, not just in the next world, but in this one.

JOAN OF ARC

Others, too, have been able to recognize the City of God in the midst of travail and sorrow. Put yourself in this scene. You've been brought up in a churchgoing family. Your nation is engaged in a war that predates your birth, a war that has divided the entire country. Rival powers and their surrogates roam the countryside, dividing and conquering. There is no safety. For your entire life the only thing you could ever count on has been the love of your family.

As you approach your teenage years, something extraordinary begins to happen. You begin to hear voices and see figures who speak to you. They identify themselves to you as angels and saints. They urge you to virtue, to faith, and to a good life. Later, they encourage you to take a role in the destiny of your people. They urge you to go to one who is identified by them as rightful king of the nation, to assist him in war, and to bring his army to victory.

You are a teenage girl, and the year is 1428. Could anything be more ridiculous than the suggestion that you might lead an army to victory? War is a man's occupation, and nation-building is not a woman's—much less a girl's—place. But you, Joan, known as "The Maiden," are sure that this is your calling. You refuse to give in until you are brought into the king's presence. You tell him something that only he would recognize as truth. His eyes are opened. He knows that you are for real. A squadron of theologians who had lost their places at the University of Paris for being on the losing side is brought in to examine you and your claims. They agree: there is something here beyond what is seen.

For your own protection you dress as a man. You take up the banner of the Lamb of God. You dare to write to nobles and generals, bishops and kings to tell them what is right and how they should respond. You lead men into battle and they are victorious. The course of the conflict shifts. The would-be king arrives at the moment of his coronation. And you are there.

A winter of forced inactivity follows. The king is cautious while you are urging action. Frustrated, you dare to act on your own, even though you foresee a bad outcome. You are captured by the enemy. Though you are a woman, you are held by men, rather than in a convent with nuns as was the custom. Though you are a sincere believer, you are put on trial before an ecclesiastical court that is compromised by its political loyalties. Through various acts of deceit, you are found guilty and condemned to death. You are burned at the stake. They grant your request that a crucifix be held before your closing eyes. You are Joan of Arc, at your death barely twenty years of age.

Within decades of your horrible death, the Church court overturns your conviction and condemnation. Much later, you are canonized and considered a heroine not only to the French people but also to Catholics everywhere. Even, perhaps, to us in our day.

There are more than a few people—some of them members of the Church—who think of the Church as old, arthritic, and unable to move, to adjust, to respond to the needs of a new time and the changing mores of the world. Many have long proclaimed the final sickness and coming death of the Church of Christ. In greater numbers than ever, it seems, they continue to do so today.

WHAT AUGUSTINE OF HIPPO AND JOAN OF ARC CAN TEACH US

Let's admit it. Things appear bleak for the Church today. We hear the dire statistics and stories of corruption and loss. But Augustine and Joan of Arc looked deeper than external circumstances—violence, corruption, division, and obstacles. They saw in God a reality that was deeper and truer than the world's. They told God's story to people of their own time, and they tell us God's story too. In genuine fashion, these saints remain our contemporaries.

This is our story as it unfolds. Ours is the tale of a body of believers and their leaders who are refreshed daily by the Word of God and the sacraments. Renewed daily, this body can respond to needs and challenges as they come up. We are in a time of innovation and revolution.

Our body has at its disposal the riches of two millennia of experience: the experience of living the Gospel in new and unforeseen circumstances. Again and again.

Innovation and revolution are nothing new to this group. To fail to innovate out of the riches of the past, to fail to begin the Christian revolution anew in each generation, to fail to re-ignite the flame of new life at each Easter: this would be unfaithful to the tradition of the Church.

Whether you see these days as being like Augustine's last on earth—with barbarians at and inside the gates—or like those of Joan with the house divided and uselessly fighting against itself—in neither case is there cause for despair. Instead, in both there is motivation for action. We want to take up the techniques of innovation with the goal of renewing the very heart of the community of faith. We may become revolutionaries, those who carry the startling words and actions of Jesus Christ to the world. What Augustine saw in his census of the City of God and what Joan saw from horseback in battle is that Jesus never grows old. And neither does his Body, which is the Church. The key is to know the way of Christ, to ingest it, and to let Jesus' life live within us to the profound point where it becomes truer to say, as Saint Paul did, that we live within Jesus' life. "I have been crucified with Christ; and it is no longer I who live, but it is Christ who lives in me" (Gal 2:19–20). If this is so, there is no dark present moment that is not suffused with the birthing hope of a bright day still to come. This is our moment to live in Christ and to do his marvelous work.

Next Steps

Prayer for Renewal of Our Perspective

Holy Lord, you make all things new. Blow away the dust and ashes of despair and discouragement. Renew our eyes, that we can see ourselves and others as Christ does. Give us your vision of the challenges and obstacles to a glorious Church in our own time. Turn us away from wars and conflicts toward the peaceful fields of harvest. Give us new minds so that we can think the fresh thoughts of our Savior as we contemplate how to bring in a bountiful harvest. Let our hearts be filled with the new wine, the love of God extending to all we encounter. Amen.

Lectio Divina

When the day of Pentecost had come, they were all together in one place. And suddenly from heaven a sound came from heaven like the rush of a mighty wind, and it filled all the house where they were sitting. And there appeared to them tongues as of fire, distributed and resting on each one of them. And they were all filled with the Holy Spirit and began to speak in other tongues, as the Spirit gave them utterance. Now there were dwelling in Jerusalem Jews, devout men from every nation under heaven. And at this sound the multitude came together and they were bewildered, because each one heard them speaking in his own language. And they were amazed and wondered, saying, "Are not all these who are speaking Galileans? And how is it that we hear, each of us in his own native language?" (Acts 2:1–8, RSV)

Application

Renewing the gifts of the Church, Sts. Augustine and Joan of Arc confronted urgent needs in their times. They led the way in seeing things new—their own vocations, the circumstances of their worlds, and the solutions to problems. Reflect today on seeing things through God's eyes. Look at yourself, your opportunities for service, and the urgent needs nearby with a confidence in God's possibilities. How may you think and act in innovative ways?

1. List the services you routinely provide for others in your life. Divide these into three categories: family, Church, community. Now determine which needs in each category are the most urgent.

2. Devise one additional service you could provide in each category, even if it necessitates deleting one for the sake of economy.

3. Think outside the box. In the Church category, imagine the most innovative addition you could bring if you had the resources that innovation required. Don't limit your imagination; what profound necessity could be met for your parish, diocese, and the global Church?

4. Consider gathering with others to begin the process of implementation or hearing how others could creatively address the issue by another means.

Questions

1. How does God's view of the circumstances of your time and place differ from your own view?

2. How does God's view of you differ from your view of yourself?

3. Based on God's view of things, how might you approach personal problems in new ways?

4. How can you extend innovative ways of seeing, speaking, and doing to others?

Notes

1. Saint Augustine, *City of God* (New York: Random House, 2010), 345.
2. Ibid., 447.

3.

To Build the Church, Build Relationships

Paul the Apostle and John Vianney

Even in an age of Internet communication, social networking, and smart phones, all with a tremendous impact on world events and on the personal lives of people everywhere, there remains a genuine transformative power in connecting face to face. Looking another child of God in the eye can still be a profound introduction, more powerful in many ways than viewing someone's well-prepared online profile complete with their best photograph.

Of course, there is a place—a place growing by leaps and bounds daily—for virtual networks of belonging. But through it all, and likely as long as human beings exist in bodily form, nothing surpasses the power and worth of coming into the presence of a dear one and greeting one another with a warm embrace.

Christianity has always had an instinct for this truth. There is little wonder in this, for ours is a faith founded on the Word becoming flesh and dwelling among us. We marvel at the mystery of Incarnation: the eternal God entering time as one of us, the invisible deity becoming visible, the untouchable Lord submitting to human touch. That human touch enabled the Lord to perform physical acts of tenderness and love, but also to suffer the violence that human touch brought as monstrous torture and an agonized death. God transformed even that violence against his Anointed One into an expression of his love for all humans, a historical moment that saves sinners like us and entitles them to bodily resurrection and eternal life in the everlasting kingdom of God. As the Church proclaims God incarnate, it affirms the worth of flesh and blood, for our bodies can powerfully express spiritual love, even as they fail and age.

In our high-tech time of virtual realities, we must not lose touch with ordinary, tangible reality. If we do, we will sacrifice much of our ability to reach others with the Gospel. That Gospel is primarily about relationship. It is about the relationship of God to God's people, witnessed and shared in what people saw and heard and experienced in the company of Jesus of Nazareth. This is what Matthew, Mark, Luke, and John have passed on to us.

PAUL THE APOSTLE

Relationship is what Paul the Apostle concentrated upon as he traveled widely to invite Jews and then Gentiles into friendship with God in and through Jesus, the Son. Having been joined in relationship with the risen Christ Jesus in extraordinary fashion, the apostle took as his own the call to build the Church by building relationships. He built community around Jesus Christ and with

Jesus Christ, person by person, conversation by conversation, letter by letter.

Short of a personal mystical revelation of the Lord, perhaps, there is still no better way to know Jesus than by coming to truly know someone whose life has been transformed by the living Christ. In that heart-to-heart encounter we find grace. The living presence of God among us is still expressed in flesh and blood today. Particularly in the mean streets and back alleys of this world the sweet grace of God is best expressed in flesh. In your body, by your words and deeds, you effectively show me Jesus. You are for me an incarnation of grace. And by that same grace I can grow to be grace for someone else. Every one of us carries out this mission in a manner absolutely unique to each, and yet we carry in common the very essence of the divine love revealed in Jesus and poured out on the Cross.

Through relationships, Paul built the local churches, greatly expanding their reach into distant lands and diverse cultures. Paul was doing what Jesus had done, but taking it further afield, as Jesus had commanded. Like Jesus, he walked the paths of his time and place and engaged men and women in conversation. In Jesus' way, Paul revealed God to his sons and daughters. One relationship at a time, Paul carried out that tradition of personal encounter. In his own time, the middle decades of the first century of the Christian era, Paul, the apostle-come-lately, did more than anyone to build Christ's Church. He understood that it is just a matter, after all, of meeting people and looking them in the eye.

John Vianney

Through the centuries many have understood the power of relationship to share the living God with others. Consider John Vianney, priest, pastor, confessor, and saint of Ars. Early in his life he was befriended by a local priest, Father Bally. That relationship transformed John Vianney's life by bringing him closer to God. Father Bally saw potential in the young man when others could not. He shepherded John Vianney to answer his call to go to seminary. When that proved unsustainable, Father Bally himself, at his own school, made sure that the future saint would come to the altar as a priest. Their relationship was God-centered, powered by the Spirit, and ultimately unstoppable in the face of serious opposition and what seemed to be intractable problems.

Once ordained and assigned to Ars, a little town almost unchurched since the French Revolution, Father Vianney set out to pastor his people by getting to know them well. He was ever-present to the people God had given him to shepherd. He entered ever more deeply into a Christ-like relationship with all those who crossed his path. As the years passed and his ministry deepened, his relationships with his people increasingly centered on the encounter between priest and penitent in the confessional. Through the latter years of his life, this pastor spent most of his days and also most of his nights hearing confessions. He became in the confessional a gateway to Jesus for others.

In the first full year of his pontificate, Saint John XXIII wrote an encyclical letter to mark the one hundredth anniversary of the death of Saint John Baptist Mary Vianney. In the opening paragraphs of the letter, Pope John recalled the several significant moments in his own life and ministry when he and John Vianney, in a real sense, crossed paths. The "good pope" himself exemplifies the vitality of sharing the Christian faith person to person. Pope John XXIII writes of Vianney:

> He proved to be a tireless worker for God, one who was wise and devoted in winning over young people and bringing families back to the standards of Christian morality, a worker who was never too tired to show an interest in the human needs of his flock, one whose own way of life was very close to theirs and who was prepared to exert every effort and make any sacrifice to establish Christian schools and to make missions available to the people: and all of these things show that Saint John M. Vianney reproduced the true image of the good shepherd in himself as he dealt with the flock entrusted to his care, for he knew his sheep, protected them from dangers, and gently but firmly looked after them.[1]

This pastoral power of relationship was a great grace to the many thousands who came to Ars to seek out Father John Vianney. For the man himself, this effort was not always easy. He became exhausted, though others may not have seen it. He struggled, but he kept going. His relationship to Jesus Christ sustained him. The love between him and his Lord gave him the power to love his people with the Heart of Christ, and he continued to do so until the day of his death.

WHAT PAUL THE APOSTLE AND JOHN VIANNEY CAN TEACH US

We all respond to faith on a personal level, and when we meet others in the world personally in the name of Christ, transformation happens. In and through those personal meetings, the Church's faith in Christ becomes a living center of the personal, familial, educational, and professional experience of real people. In these relationships of faithful love, these incarnational networks, we experience what the Church really is, we realize that here is where we belong, and we extend to others the invitation to join us.

Recently the power of relationships in Christ has been revealed in Pope Francis's approach to his service as pope. He has caught the attention of a hungry world. He communicates person to person, to the great and the small, that Jesus Christ lives, that the Gospel is a way of life, and that the Church is the community of those who "are in the midst of a love story—each one of us is a link in this chain of love."[2]

In our relationships, we can participate in this great love story, strengthening the chain. To do so, as Pope Francis teaches, is to understand what the Church really is, what is its power, and what will ensure its existence until Christ comes again at the end of the age.

Next Steps

Prayer to Build Relationships

Jesus, you said that your followers would fish for people, that we would carry on your work of reuniting them with your Father and introducing them to the kingdom of heaven. I seek to obey you in reaching out, but I need your help to put people first in my life. Please give me the same Spirit that enabled you, Saint Paul, and Saint John Vianney to walk and speak the truth to all. Give me grace to connect with integrity that I may bear fruit to your glory. Give me the gift of listening to understand deeply, as Saint Vianney did. Give me knowledge and courage to walk and speak as your ambassador in places where you are unknown or even despised, as Saint Paul did. But, most of all, Lord, give me the love you had for the many who came to you, the many who were too busy for you, and even the many who played a role in putting you to death. You loved them all, as you love all the people I encounter in my days. Open my heart to others. Open my mind to see opportunities to invite others into genuine relationships that honor you. Amen.

Lectio Divina

That very day two of them were going to a village named Emmaus, about seven miles from Jerusalem, and talking with each other about all these things that had happened. While they were talking and discussing together, Jesus himself drew near and went with them. But their eyes were kept from recognizing him. And he said to them, "What is this conversation which you are holding with each other as you walk?" And they stood still, looking sad. Then one of them, named Cleopas, answered him, "Are you the only visitor to Jerusalem who does not know the things that have happened there in these days?" And he said to them, "What things?" And they said to him, "Concerning Jesus of Nazareth, who was a prophet mighty in deed and word before God and all the people, and how our chief priests and rulers delivered him up to be condemned to death, and crucified him. But we had hoped that he was the one to redeem Israel. Yes, and besides all this, it is now the third day since this happened. Moreover, some women of our company amazed us. They were at the tomb early in the morning and did not find his body; and they came back saying they had even seen a vision of angels, who said that he was alive. Some of those who were with us went to the tomb, and found it just as the women had said; but him they did not see." And he said to them, "O foolish men, and slow of heart to believe all that the prophets have spoken! Was it not necessary that the Christ should suffer these things and enter into his glory?" And beginning with Moses and all the prophets, he interpreted to them in all the scriptures the things concerning himself.

So they drew near to the village to which they were going. He appeared to be going further, but they constrained him, saying, "Stay with us, for it is toward evening and the day is now far spent." So he went in to stay with them. When he was at table with them, he took the bread and blessed, and broke it, and gave it to them. And their eyes were opened and they recognized him; and he vanished out of their sight. They said to each other, "Did not our hearts burn within us while he talked to us on the road, while he opened to us the scriptures?" And they rose that same hour and returned to Jerusalem; and they found the eleven gathered together and those who were with them, who said, "The Lord has risen indeed, and has appeared to Simon!" Then they told what had happened on the road, and how he was known to them in the breaking of the bread. (Lk 24:13–35, RSV)

Application

1. Take stock of your own relationship to Jesus Christ. Look for what's missing or left uncultivated and ask Jesus to remedy that need.

2. Consider your family or community and choose one relationship that has been left untended or is in need of rejuvenation. Devise an approach to heal and build up that relationship.

3. Determine the greatest need in your community or the greatest opportunity for healing and renewal in love. Think about how you can work with others to bring God's love into that situation.

Questions

1. Can you think of one way in which your faith life intersects with your public life?

2. Are you open to new relationships?

3. Do you seek to listen to and truly understand those you encounter?

4. Do you dare to share your authentic self with others, even beyond your immediate family?

5. Do those who know you know that you love God?

6. Can you be honest about your faults and shortcomings?

7. Can you apologize to others for things you have done that hurt them?

8. Can you forgive others and forget the hurt they have done you?

9. Do you invite God into your relationships?

10. Can you think of one way you are privileged to glorify the Lord by your life?

Notes

1. Pope John XXIII, *Sacerdotii nostri primordial*, 63.

2. Pope Francis, Homily, April 24, 2013, http://www .catholicnewsagency.com/news/church-is-a-love-story -pope-francis-says/ (accessed February 28, 2014).

4.

Make Use of
New Technologies

Isidore and Fulton J. Sheen

Early in life we are highly adaptive and adaptable. When parents bring an infant home, they watch it assimilating new things hour to hour and day to day. The child's eyes follow movement or turn to locate the source of sound. The head swivels toward stimuli, especially faces. Before you know it, the little one is communicating feelings and desires through his or her expressions, sounds, and gestures. Soon the child is sitting up, crawling, taking first steps, and racing about to discover what's new. When the child grasps some new idea or grasps some new thing, he or she immediately puts it to his or her own purposes. At the same time, the child is constantly adapting himself or herself to a rapidly changing understanding of the world.

New communities possess the characteristics of an infant. The pioneers who set out for the American West were ready to use whatever resources they found around them or adapt whatever they had brought with them to establish new homes, farms, pasture lands, mines, businesses, and a myriad of new possibilities. They had fresh eyes to see what was around them, and they were open to envisioning how what was given could be used to bring about something still unseen.

The first generations of Christians following Jesus' death and resurrection were the same kind of open and alive entrepreneurs. Philip the deacon recognized a seemingly chance meeting with a foreign government official along the road as an opportunity to share faith in Jesus and to bring new life to that visitor. The Acts of the Apostles tells the story of Philip hearing a court official of the queen of the Ethiopians reading the prophet Isaiah in his chariot. Philip said, "'Do you understand what you are reading?' The official replied, 'How can I unless some instructs me?'" So Philip climbed up into the chariot and showed him that the passage about the sheep being led to the slaughter referred to Jesus. After that, the official ordered the chariot to stop and had Philip baptize him immediately (Acts 8:26–39). Philip had adapted himself to a unique opportunity with openness that was prompted by the Holy Spirit.

Paul the Apostle was tireless in his voyages of faith, going wherever he was called. He would engage anyone willing to listen as he shared the marvelous gift of faith in Christ that had been revealed to him in unexpected and extraordinary fashion. Paul was a stranger in many strange lands. The concept of missionary outreach, especially to the Gentiles, was completely new in the world. Paul was an inveterate innovator. Paul understood that the people he was trying to reach with the good news about Jesus were aching to know this news and, once they had received it, they would adapt to it and grow in the love of God. They would be saved from sin and death and receive eternal life. A great new thing had come into the world, and the whole world was beginning to adapt to it.

Unfortunately for us, we do not remain as fresh and open as we were as babies. Not only our bodies, but also our minds and imaginations can become stiff and unresponsive. More than a few of those towns founded with energy and determination in the western plains of the United States were abandoned after a slow and painful demise. The energy that created them slowly ran out of their streets, and the expectation of new things and openness to innovation simply faded away. They became ghost towns.

The Church, though founded by our Divine Savior who remains with it and will sustain it until the end of time, is, nevertheless, a human institution as well. The Second Vatican Council noted the dual nature of the Church in the second paragraph of its first promulgated document: "It is of the essence of the Church that she be both human and divine."[1] In its human nature, the Church, like any human being, can grow creaky and cranky, her arteries closed or partially closed to the rushing lifeblood of divine grace.

If and when the Church is limited by things as they are, if the status quo becomes a wall blocking from sight the next great thing to which God is calling his people, then we have a Church in crisis. Each generation has a difficult, but vitally necessary, spiritual exercise before it. We must open our eyes and ears widely to see what is happening in our own time. Do we recognize that ours is a time of crisis? Are there ways in which we are stuck? Have we stopped seeing opportunities to make Jesus come alive in our generation, as Philip made Jesus come alive to the government official in the chariot? If we do see that we are missing things, that we are bound by ideas and practices that tie us to some arbitrary past and hinder us in the present, we can recognize our need to be shaken out of it so that we may receive that old but ever new power of the Spirit as Samson did. We can turn back to our first condition of openness and adaptation to the present.

We don't have to return to the womb to be renewed in our energies. Remember what Jesus told Nicodemus when the elderly Pharisee puzzled about the suggestion that he must be born again. Jesus said to him:

> No one can enter the kingdom of God without being born of water and Spirit. What is born of flesh is flesh, and what is born of spirit is spirit. Do not be amazed that I told you, "You must be born from above." The wind blows where it wills, and you can hear the sound it makes, but you do not know where it comes from or where it goes; so it is with everyone who is born of the Spirit. (Jn 3:5–8, NAB)

What do those words mean to us? They mean we can become infants fresh in the face of life again. God's beloved people, each one of us, can—Jesus says *must*—be born again.

A dynamic Church challenges itself constantly. A dynamic Church continuously grows and innovates. Two bishops of the past, Isidore and Fulton J. Sheen, saw with fresh eyes the possibility for sharing the faith inherent in new technologies of their time. They grasped these new tools and placed them at the service of the faith.

Isidore

Isidore succeeded his elder brother as bishop of Seville at the dawn of the seventh century. His diocese, like all Spain, consisted of people divided between the passing culture of the Roman Empire and that of the conquering Visigoths. It was ultimately futile to call the newcomers (now present for some two centuries) barbarians. It would be much more useful, Isidore saw, to find a way to unite the two peoples and cultures. Isidore was looking at his world with fresh eyes. Those eyes, like his mind, remained open, fresh, and clear for the almost four decades of his episcopacy.

The new tool that Isidore fashioned and used to great effect was a book known as *Etymologiae*. For the first time anywhere a leader in the Church of Christ provided for people a summary of all knowledge, a kind of encyclopedia. In this monumental undertaking Isidore was energized by the conviction, it seems, that sharing all that is known would reveal the unity underlying fragmentary perspectives. Readers of his *Etymologiae* through later centuries note the presence there of both the ancient Roman ways and those of the newer rulers of the land. In his writing and in person, Isidore saw the possibilities of his day and seized them. Undeterred by the past and the problems of the present, he set out to share the faith. In our time, during the papacy of John Paul II, Isidore was chosen as the patron saint of the Internet. No doubt had he lived in the late twentieth and twenty-first centuries the bishop of Seville would have been blogging and tweeting the faith to all with the ears, and technologies, to hear.

FULTON J. SHEEN

In our own recent past is the figure of the Venerable Fulton J. Sheen, bishop of the airwaves, both radio and television. Trained as a philosopher and theologian, Fulton Sheen used his intellect and wit to communicate profound truths with new media to millions. Early in his ministry, he recognized the possibility that radio, and later television, held to reach many more men and women than had ever been reached before. On the radio he spoke to four million listeners a week over a two decade-long period of broadcasting. When he moved to New York, became a bishop, and began broadcasting on television in 1951, viewers of the program eventually reached some thirty million. This Catholic bishop, speaking about the faith in every aspect of living, became the biggest thing on the small screen.

Archbishop Sheen, whose cause for sainthood is well underway in our day, had the skills of a wise communicator. He was able to translate what might have seemed to be distant or complex ideas into the language and the experience of people's actual lives. Others had this talent as well, in his time and always. But like Saint Isidore, Bishop Fulton Sheen also had eyes wide open to the possibilities of the technologies of his time. We can assume that everyone in the Catholic Church of his time listened to the radio and watched, or at least knew about, television. But Fulton Sheen heard and saw in these amazing technologies new tools for evangelization, and he stepped up and made them work for the Church.

What Isidore and Fulton J. Sheen Can Teach Us

Much more dramatically than during the time of Isidore or even Bishop Sheen, in our own time new communication technologies are proliferating almost daily, all with great potential for evangelization. More than ever before new technologies present unheard-of opportunities to spread the truth about Jesus' crucifixion and resurrection. In our time and in the decades to come there is more potential growth in the preaching of the Gospel than in all the time since Jesus' crucifixion and resurrection. Can we believe it? Do we have the fresh eyes needed to see where God is leading us?

NEXT STEPS

Prayer for Openness to Adapting Technologies

Father, in our time, as in all times, you are calling many to the kingdom of Heaven, where you live with your Son, our Lord, Jesus Christ, in the unity of the Holy Spirit. Help us to be instruments of your call to the immense and growing human population of our world today. Like people of Jesus' time, these people are like sheep without a shepherd unless they come to you. Send your Holy Spirit to give us fresh eyes to see the needs and the opportunities for the Gospel in our time. Give us open minds to take up and use new communication technologies that will broadcast your Word far and wide, even to the ends of the earth. Let us be inspired by those who have adapted the technologies of the past for the proliferation of the Gospel. Amen.

Lectio Divina

Then an angel of the Lord said to Philip, "Get up and go toward the south to the road that goes down from Jeru-salem to Gaza." (This is a wilderness road.) So he got up and went. Now there was an Ethiopian eunuch, a court official of the Candace, queen of the Ethiopians, in charge of her entire treasury. He had come to Jerusalem to wor-ship and was returning home; seated in his chariot, he was reading the prophet Isaiah. Then the Spirit said to Philip, "Go over to this chariot and join it." So Philip ran up to it and heard him reading the prophet Isaiah. He asked, "Do you understand what you are reading?" He replied, "How can I, unless someone guides me?" And he invited Philip to get in and sit beside him. Now the passage of the scripture that he was reading was this:

> Like a sheep he was led to the slaughter,
> and like a lamb silent before its shearer,
> so he does not open his mouth.
> In his humiliation justice was denied him.
> Who can describe his generation?
> For his life is taken away from the earth.

The eunuch asked Philip, "About whom, may I ask you, does the prophet say this, about himself or about someone else?" Then Philip began to speak, and starting with this scripture, he proclaimed to him the good news about Jesus. As they were going along the road, they came to some water; and the eunuch said, "Look, here is water! What is to prevent me from being baptized?" He commanded the chariot to stop, and both of them, Philip and the eunuch, went down into the water, and Philip baptized him. When they came up out of the water, the Spirit of the Lord snatched Philip away; the eunuch saw him no more, and went on his way rejoicing. (Acts 8:26–39)

Application

1. Identify what you consider to be the three major crisis points in the Church today.

2. Identify what you consider to be the three major crisis points of your own daily practice of the faith.

3. Reflect on your own uses of technologies, their positive and negative effects on your personal life.

4. List some current examples of the effective use of technology by the Church in the United States.

5. Reflect on your organization's uses of technologies, pro and con.

Questions

1. In your own parish or campus, diocese or ministry, how might technology be employed for a more powerful evangelization?

2. Have you considered doing research into how other organizations, religious or secular, are using technologies effectively to achieve their missions?

3. Have you considered starting or joining a multidisciplinary team to explore technologies in search of creative solutions and applications in your organization?

4. Do you or the people in your organization have outside contacts who have expertise in technologies and would be willing to advise you?

5. Are there ways to increase the positive and reduce the negative effects of technologies in your organization?

Note

1. *Sacrosanctum concilium,* 2, http://www.vatican.va/archive/hist_councils/ii_vatican_council/documents/vat-ii_const_19631204_sacrosanctum-concilium_en.html (accessed February 27, 2014).

5.

EMBRACE THE CROSS

Pope John Paul II
and Edith Stein

When Pope John Paul II beatified Edith Stein in Cologne on May 1, 1987, he spoke these words:

> We bow down before the testimony of the life and death of Edith Stein, an outstanding daughter of Israel and at the same time a daughter of the Carmelite Order, Sister Teresa Benedicta of the Cross, a personality who united within her rich life a dramatic synthesis of our century. It was the synthesis of a history full of deep wounds that are still hurting ... and also the synthesis of the full truth about man. All this came together in a single heart that remained restless and unfulfilled until it finally found rest in God.

These two extraordinary lives met again when John Paul canonized her in St. Peter's Square in October 1998.

In less obvious fashion, Karol Wojtyla and Edith Stein intersected in the midst of the century they shared. Each one confronted the totalitarian terror of the last century in their own lives and in their own bodies. As a

young man, the future priest and pope was struck and
seriously injured by a truck of the German occupiers in
his native Poland in 1944. He studied for ordination in
the secret underground seminary run during the war by
the Archdiocese of Krakow.

A brilliant philosopher, Edith Stein converted from
Judaism and was baptized Catholic in 1922. She entered
the Carmelites in 1933, taking the religious name Sister
Teresa Benedicta. When the Nazi terror became vicious
in 1938, the Carmelite community moved her from
Cologne to their convent in the Netherlands for safety.
While World War II was raging throughout Europe, the
Dutch Catholic bishops issued a strong anti-Nazi state-
ment. In response the Nazis arrested all Jewish converts
to Catholicism in that nation. Edith Stein and her sister
were taken captive, and Sister Teresa Benedicta died in
the concentration camp at Auschwitz on August 9, 1942.

What Pope John Paul said of Edith Stein on the
occasion of his declaration of her sainthood might be
said as well of him: "The mystery of the Cross gradually
enveloped her whole life. . . . Sister Teresa Benedicta not
only wrote profoundly about the 'science of the Cross';
she was thoroughly trained in the school of the Cross."

Many of our contemporaries would like to silence
the Cross. But in silence the Cross is most eloquent,
for it speaks of the nature of love. Suffering can be an
instrument to express love, deepening it, proving it. Love
makes suffering fruitful. Through her experience of the
Cross, Edith Stein was able to open the way to a new
encounter with the God of Abraham, Isaac, and Jacob,
the Father of our Lord Jesus Christ. Faith and the Cross
proved inseparable to her.

WHAT POPE JOHN PAUL II AND EDITH STEIN CAN TEACH US

For both of these monumental figures, the Cross that filled and defined their lives was not in itself an end. The acceptance of what it cost to confront suffering and evil led them to the Cross and through the Cross to new life, as it does in the Paschal Mystery of the life of the Christ. As for Christ, so too for Christians. The Cross energized them through their entire life experience, especially in their most difficult moments. In a fashion fully integrated with the persons their lives had forged them to become—a man and a woman of strength, constancy, and commitment—Pope John Paul II and Edith Stein show us how to develop an inner core of strength that provides us with the resources and principles that guide our lives and open a way to positive change. Each of us has the capability and the responsibility to do the same.

Saint John Paul II possessed the inner strength to challenge both the Church and our culture with probing questions throughout his papacy of more than a quarter century: What is the origin and purpose of the human person? How can we have complete confidence in God and move forward without fear? What is true freedom? How can religion and science purify each other? Why is marriage and family so key to the human family? How can young people more clearly hear and respond to the voice and love of Christ? Such questions, centered on faith, on what it means to live a human life graced in and by Jesus Christ, and on how to take responsibility for one another, for society, and for the times which we share, allowed him to inspire the Church to prepare for and to enter the third millennium of Christianity.

Edith Stein, by the choices that shaped her life, shares the pathway that embraces the saving will of God for his people Israel, and through Israel for the entire world in the person of Christ. She mirrors God's faithfulness in the faithful sacrifice of her life at Carmel and at Auschwitz. In both she was moved by profound love that led her to the Cross.

Both of these trailblazing figures teach us how to be faithful when confronting situations that challenge our faith and require a cost for that fidelity. Their witness calls us to act with confidence in expressing our faith, but at the same time to be open to new understandings. We do this when we:

- Point out the strengths of believing and living the Catholic life: confidence in what has given you life and shown you saving truth will attract others to faith.

- Maintain utmost charity in all our relationships: love opens the door to mutual understanding and to progress in harmony.

- Do not be afraid to look at other systems of belief: hold your own belief firmly while seeking to understand and appreciate what others hold sacred.

- Maintain dialogue with other Christian communities and religious traditions: nothing is gained by the refusal to engage with others, and much is possible when people of good will enter into conversation.

The mission of Jesus led him to the Cross and through the Cross to glory at the right hand of the Father. His faithfulness to the Father's will brought to humanity the gift of the Spirit, the Paraclete, with us and in us. That same mission and faithfulness are passed through the Holy Spirit to disciples of Jesus Christ in every age. No one will rejuvenate a mission more effectively than one who listens well and learns from others in order to reinvigorate the Church. Edith Stein and John Paul II demonstrated this truth in the midst of a harrowing, confusing, and difficult time. It is more than possible that we can do the same in our time.

NEXT STEPS

Prayer to Embrace the Cross of Christ

Almighty Father of our Lord Jesus Christ, give me your Holy Spirit that I may know you and live in you every day and every hour. I offer my life to you, Lord, that I may do your will and bring glory to you. In particular, I pray that like Jesus and like the many, many great saints of the Church, I may embrace the Cross, knowing that in my suffering according to your will I am walking in the way of your love. Let me rejoice in the Cross, for it joins me to you and it will bear fruit for the good of others as they too come to know you, love you, and serve you. In addition to the Cross, I ask you to strengthen whatever spiritual gifts you confer upon me. Let me use those gifts in cooperation with others who have received differing gifts. This is the plan for your Church, Lord. Let your perfect will be done. Amen.

Lectio Divina

[Jesus said,] "I tell you, my friends, do not be afraid of those who kill the body but after that can do no more. I shall show you whom to fear. Be afraid of the one who after killing has the power to cast into Gehenna; yes, I tell you, be afraid of that one. Are not five sparrows sold for two small coins? Yet not one of them has escaped the notice of God. Even the hairs of your head have all been counted. Do not be afraid. You are worth more than many sparrows.

"I tell you, everyone who acknowledges me before others the Son of Man will acknowledge before the angels of God. But whoever denies me before others will be denied before the angels of God. Everyone who speaks a word against the Son of Man will be forgiven, but the one who blasphemes against the holy Spirit will not be forgiven. When they take you before synagogues and before rulers and authorities, do not worry about how or what your defense will be or about what you are to say. For the holy Spirit will teach you at that moment what you should say."

✳ ✳ ✳

He said to his disciples, "Therefore I tell you, do not worry about your life and what you will eat, or about your body and what you will wear. For life is more than food and the body more than clothing. Notice the ravens: they do not sow or reap; they have neither storehouse nor barn, yet God feeds them. How much more important are you than birds! Can any of you by worrying add a moment to your lifespan? If even the smallest things are beyond your control, why are you anxious about the rest?

"Notice how the flowers grow. They do not toil or spin. But I tell you, not even Solomon in all his splendor was dressed like one of them. If God so clothes the grass in the field that grows today and is thrown into the oven tomorrow, will he not much more provide for you, O you of little faith? As for you, do not seek what you are to eat and what you are to drink, and do not worry anymore. All the nations of the world seek for these things, and your Father knows that you need them. Instead, seek his kingdom, and these other things will be given you besides.

"Do not be afraid any longer, little flock, for your Father is pleased to give you the kingdom. Sell your belongings and give alms. Provide money bags for yourselves that do not wear out, an inexhaustible treasure in heaven that no thief can reach nor moth destroy. For where your treasure is, there also will your heart be." (Lk 12:4–12; 22–34, NAB)

Application

1. The cross that Jesus carried, which became his throne of suffering and the altar of his great sacrifice, is inseparable from our life as Christians. Even before we are baptized, the Church and our parents marked us with the cross on our foreheads. Consider how the mystery of suffering has marked your life up to now. Make a list of your "crosses."

2. Saint Rose of Lima said, "Apart from the cross there is no other ladder by which we may get to heaven." The struggles of life can be strange gifts, in the sense that they open us up to the mystery of God's ever-present love. As you have carried life's crosses, see in retrospect the graces shared and growth in your baptismal call to holiness.

3. Hold a cross in your hands and ask for the faith, hope, and love necessary to embrace whatever you are facing in your life right now. Compose a short prayer that you can use when life gets very tough.

Questions

1. On your life's journey, what has been the most profound cross to which you have been nailed? What is your cross today?

2. The cross causes us to die to self, and to surrender ourselves into God's hands. How has your biggest cross been the paradoxical means to a fuller life even now?

3. We cannot carry the cross by our own power. We need God's help! How has that divine help manifested itself in small and dramatic ways over the years?

4. If you could pick your own cross to carry this year, what would it be? Would its burden be light or heavy?

6.

ENCOURAGE EVERYDAY HEROISM

Dorothy Day and Francis of Assisi

They each befriended poverty, though their perspectives differed. He embraced it as a way to follow Christ more closely. She lamented the suffering it brought to so many men, women, and children. Yet at the same time, in solidarity with them she too embraced it. She lived it in their company in all its messiness and want and pain. And there, Dorothy Day too, as Francis of Assisi had before her, found a ready path to Jesus' side.

What marks both of these Christians, living in vastly different times and cultures, is this: both of them committed fully to what they believed, and they lived it every day. Whatever that commitment asked. However silly it might look. However dangerous. However likely to alienate those with power.

Neither of them relied on power. Paradoxically they relied on weakness, on emptying themselves into Christ, or Christ into themselves. But their goal was actually to change the world. Nothing less. And, of course, they did.

Dorothy Day

Dorothy Day believed, as she often said and wrote, that the way to change the world was "little by little." There was no use in saying, "I cannot do this; I am only one person." Rather, her byword was this: "I am one person; I can do this much." She put it this way:

> What we would like to do is change the world— make it a little simpler for people to feed, clothe, and shelter themselves as God intended them to do. And, by fighting for better conditions, by crying out unceasingly for the rights of the workers, the poor, of the destitute—the rights of the worthy and the unworthy poor, in other words—we can, to a certain extent, change the world; we can work for the oasis, the little cell of joy and peace in a harried world. We can throw our pebble in the pond and be confident that its ever widening circle will reach around the world. We repeat, there is nothing we can do but love, and, dear God, please enlarge out hearts to love each other, to love our neighbor, to love our enemy as our friend.[1]

"There is nothing we can do but love." Embedded in these words is a creed that can alter human reality and carry it light years closer to the divine reality which has brought us into being and called us together as the Church.

Francis of Assisi

We have many fewer words of Francis than we do of Dorothy Day, who was after all, among many other things, a writer in the modern era of print publications. But what we do hear from Francis across more than eight centuries rings out loud and clear: "Sanctify yourself," he said, "and you will sanctify society." And another time: "We have been called to heal wounds, to unite what has fallen apart, and to bring home those who have lost their way." We are called to change a world that is wounded, fractured, and lost.

These two impoverished servants of God and others did not intend nor consider themselves to be doing anything extraordinary. They heard the voice of Jesus Christ in the Gospel and it transformed their hearts immediately and then continued to transform their hearts as long as they lived. They looked around and saw societies, in both the twelfth and twentieth centuries, that looked as though God had never spoken, nor acted, nor called human persons to speak and act with him. But Dorothy and Francis knew that, in fact, God was still calling men and women to allow him to speak and work through them to renew the world. He had been doing so all along.

They thought that God's call and their response was something ordinary. It was, after all, simply obedience to the call of Christ to follow him, and who could match his love? But Francis's service of the Lord was so extraordinary that Francis of Assisi remains, all these generations after his death, one of the most widely known and respected disciples of Jesus who has ever drawn breath. And Dorothy Day also endures as an exceptional instance of God's reaching gently, deeply, and persistently into a life; transforming that life, and through that transformation, helping and even transforming countless others.

We may be tempted to call them heroes. For they heard the tiny whispering voice of God and responded with deep commitment and practical daily action. These

two and the many others of whom we have already
spoken truly are heroes of the faith. And yet, there is
every indication that they did not consider themselves
to be heroes. Dorothy said, in a famous phrase that later
became the title of a documentary done on her life,
"Don't call me a saint. I don't want to be dismissed that
easily." A less well-known phrase attributed to Saint
Francis captured the same sentiment. He is supposed to
have said, "Don't canonize me too soon. I'm perfectly
capable of fathering a child." In other words, he knew
he was capable of breaking his vows he had made before
God and the Church. Even as he struggled toward holiness, he never lost his sense that he was a sinner.

What Dorothy Day and Francis of Assisi Can Teach Us

What if we responded to God's call as Dorothy and Francis did? Imagine a Church and a world in which more
than a few of the souls living in each generation were as
committed to faith and love in action as Francis of Assisi
or Dorothy Day. If we can't imagine that, we are called to
grow our imaginations and to strengthen our faith. We
are called to broaden our vision of what we see as possible and what we see as needed. Why? Because this is
God's call; this is the Church that God is building in our
own generation, if we have ears to hear it. Our choice is
either to sign on to work with the Father of Jesus Christ
in the power of their Spirit in this terrestrial building
project, or to pass it off as a crazy dream, a pious wish.

 If the father of the Franciscans or the founder of
the Catholic Worker Movement are heroes, then we are
called to be heroes as well. The call to be heroic in the
way that they have been is so universal a call, as the

Second Vatican Council reminds us, as to be absolutely ordinary.

Do you believe in Jesus the Christ? Have you heard the Gospel? Have you been baptized? Do you understand your life as an ongoing dialogue between your heart and the heart of God? Then you are called to be the next Dorothy Day and the next Francis of Assisi. It is true. It is real. It is possible. And it is needed. If we accept that call, the present crisis in the life of the Church will be rapidly transformed into a lasting season of joy for all who call the earth home.

Next Steps

Prayer for Authenticity

Lord, Jesus Christ, I seek you, believing that even to seek you is to find you, for that is your promise. Strengthen my faith and give me ears to hear your call to authenticity, not just once, but every day. You became a human being to show us what a man or woman should be, full of love and truth. You give us gifts to follow you and to serve others as you did. You call me to be authentically Christian, inwardly and outwardly. Give me the courage to hear and obey your call. Amen.

Lectio Divina

He also told this parable to some who trusted in themselves that they were righteous and regarded others with contempt: "Two men went up to the temple to pray, one a Pharisee and the other a tax-collector. The Pharisee, standing by himself, was praying thus, 'God, I thank you that I am not like other people: thieves, rogues, adulterers, or even like this tax-collector. I fast twice a week; I give a tenth of all my income.' But the tax-collector, standing far off, would not even look up to heaven, but was beating his breast and saying, 'God, be merciful to me, a sinner!' I tell you, this man went down to his home justified rather than the other; for all who exalt themselves will be humbled, but all who humble themselves will be exalted." (Lk 18:9–14)

Application

1. List the heroes of your life, individuals who have inspired you to the greatness for which you were created.

2. Consider how through your Confirmation and in other ways the Holy Spirit has strengthened you and given you gifts to share.

Questions

1. What are your spiritual gifts?

2. How can you actualize them today and tomorrow? A year from now?

3. Who are the "poor" in your life?

4. What responsibility do you have for them?

NOTES

1. Dorothy Day, *Dorothy Day: Selected Writings*, ed. Robert Ellsberg (Maryknoll, NY: Orbis Books, 2005), 98.

7.

BE GROUNDED, STEADFAST IN THE TRUTH

Athanasius and Mother Teresa

During four challenging and formative years, I had the honor of walking daily through the doors of the Pontifical North American College. It is situated on extraterritorial Vatican property on the side of Rome's Janiculum Hill and enjoys a spectacular view of the dome of St. Peter's Basilica. "The College" is the Eternal City's house of formation for American seminarians under the auspices of the bishops of the United States. That front door, fondly referred to as *"Firmum Est,"* brings the resident or guest past the seal of the college inlaid on the marble floor and its revered Latin motto, which in English means "Steadfast Is My Heart." Speaking of that motto, Saint John Paul II once said these words to us:

> Dear brothers: as you reflect and give thanks, and as you rededicate yourselves for what lies ahead, remember always: "Jesus Christ is the same yesterday, today, and forever" (Heb 13:8). It is to him that your lives belong. He alone fully explains the past history, present existence, and future destiny. . . . And

71

> it is in his love that you must be steadfast, in order
> to serve God's people in America: the heart of each
> one of you steadfast forever in his love, according
> to the motto of your College: *Firmum est cor meum!*"[1]

In that time and place, we were inspired to discern God's call within the broad context of those who had gone before us, not only the many priests prepared for service there on the Janiculum Hill, but also Sts. Peter and Paul, the two Apostolic heroes of Rome who held steadfastly unto death to the truth of that one, holy, and catholic faith. In the words of the ancient apologist Tertullian, "The blood of the martyrs is the seed of the Church."[2]

For all of us, there are brothers and sisters who have walked this way before us and who can show us the authentic path. Their lives were profoundly marked by steadfast faith. At the same time, they experienced frustration and suffering, what the tradition would call a sharing in the Cross of Christ throughout life. Yet somehow they did much more than survive. Although their times and circumstances might differ from our own, like us they are human persons who experienced fully human lives, lives both of faith and suffering. When we look deeply into their past we can see new light shed on our present experiences and on our future hopes.

ATHANASIUS

Take Athanasius, for example. The fourth-century bishop of Alexandria has been acclaimed through all the generations since as one of the most gifted defenders of the faith; particularly as the defender of the doctrine of the full humanity of Jesus Christ, the second Person of the Trinity.

Before the Council of Nicaea had yet defined that Christ is "of one substance" with God the Father, Athanasius, as a very young man, had already written two major treatises in defense of the faith. By all accounts he was smart, courageous, and persistent, and he possessed a great sense of humor. He would certainly need all of the gifts God had given him.

On his deathbed, Alexander, his bishop and friend whom he assisted at the Council of Nicaea, recommended Athanasius as his successor. In consequence, in the year 326, when he was only about the age of a graduate student in our time, Athanasius was unanimously elected Bishop and Patriarch. Those believers who refused to accept the doctrine about Christ from the Council of Nicaea, nominally led by the priest Arius, were determined in their opposition to Athanasius. Over the next several decades, Athanasius was exiled five times from his diocese. He was judged before councils of bishops, popes, and emperors—sometimes exonerated and sometimes found guilty. Athanasius's fortunes waxed and waned throughout those decades, dependent upon whether the truth that the Council of Nicaea had formulated about the person of Jesus Christ was received by the powers that be.

Through it all, Athanasius was steadfast. His five periods of enforced absence from the people of Alexandria varied in length from months to years. He remained confident each time that he would return home. He defended his theological position before friend and foe, again and again, with unbending courage. He wrote masterful works on the Incarnation, against the teachings of the Arians, on the life of Saint Antony of the Desert, and more. There is no evidence that he ever wavered, publicly or privately, in his defense of the Church's faith in the Incarnation of Christ. And after a long life of drama and adventure, he died quietly in bed, at home, in the city he had guided in the faith for most of his life.

Athanasius might have been excused if he had reconciled himself to mere survival. For some that would have sufficed. But for this believer and bishop, just to survive was never enough. For him, living meant continuing to proclaim without ceasing the truth of Christ to the world. As long as he lived, he exhibited untiring commitment to the Gospel and to Christ's people. He refused to lie down and die before God called him. No opposition, no suffering, no violence, no loneliness, no uncertainty was a match to this man's resolute living-out of his faith in Jesus. In circumstances that might convince many of us to run for our lives, Athanasius found deep inner fulfillment as one baptized into the death and resurrection of Jesus Christ.

Some might be tempted to discount the significance of Athanasius to us and to the Church in our time simply because he lived long ago in an earlier Church, in a very different age. But we should not discount the importance of what he accomplished. He upheld the truth we hold today, the truth of the Incarnation, that Jesus Christ is the Word made flesh. For Athanasius understood that it makes all the difference to believers to know who Jesus is, the divine Son of God, of one substance with the Father.

Athanasius worked and taught in a time of tumult, radical change, and uncertainty about the future of both Church and society. In other words, his time has a lot in common with our own. And it is a wonderful thing that lives of courageous faith like that of Athanasius are still being lived today.

MOTHER TERESA

Take Mother Teresa, for example, still within reach of memory for many of us. Her name recalls for us her valiant service to "the poorest of the poor" in the name of Jesus. Hers is the story of a "call within a call," as in the 1940s she went from the Sisters of Loretto Convent into the streets of Calcutta, India, to minister directly to those on the brink of death. Her heroic compassion caught the attention and admiration of people everywhere, Christians and non-Christians, believers and non-believers, throughout the world. Even vocal non-believers in God, such as Christopher Hitchens, found it impossible to ignore her example. By the 1970s this tiny woman was known everywhere, her voice ringing out in defense of those who had no voice.

In 1979, receiving the Nobel Peace Prize, she said to those gathered in Oslo:

> I was surprised in the West to see so many young boys and girls given into drugs, and I tried to find out why—why is it like that, and the answer was: Because there is no one in the family to receive them. Father and mother are so busy they have no time. Young parents are in some institution and the child takes back to the street and gets involved in something. We are talking of peace. These are things that break peace, but I feel the greatest destroyer of peace today is abortion, because it is a direct war, a direct killing—direct murder by the mother herself. And we read in the Scripture, for God says very clearly: Even if a mother could forget her child—I will not forget you—I have carved you in the palm of my hand. We are carved in the palm of his hand, so close to Him that unborn child has been carved in

the hand of God. And that is what strikes me most, the beginning of that sentence, that even if a mother could forget, something impossible—but even if she could forget—I will not forget you.[3]

Meek, unprepossessing, and seeking nothing for herself, Mother Teresa was able to speak with bold sincerity everywhere she went. She spoke the truth of Jesus' presence among the poor today and always. She spoke of poverty she experienced in the Third World, as we called it then, and in the developed countries of the planet. And she received a hearing in the public square, even as she said things that others were not speaking. Many called her a saint even while she lived, and continued to do so after her death, even before the documentation of her life was collected and published as a part of the process of her cause for canonization as an official saint of the Church.

Mother Teresa died in 1997. In 2003, the postulator of her cause, Father Brian Kolodiejchuk, M.C., published *The Soul of Mother Teresa: Hidden Aspects of Her Interior Life.* This was followed in 2007 by a full-length book containing never-before-seen letters of Mother Teresa and a commentary by Father Kolodiejchuk. The book's title, *Come Be My Light,* was taken from words she said were spoken to her by Jesus as he called her to the ministry of the Missionaries of Charity. He said, "Come be my light."

Her letters caused a tremendous uproar when they were made public. Major news organizations and media outlets produced stories on Mother Teresa when the book was released. Mother Teresa had asked that these letters be destroyed. She feared how others would receive them. She feared that they might challenge the faith of some. The letters reveal a deep darkness and almost despair in her soul, virtually unbroken from 1949 until her death in 1997. While she built the Missionaries of Charity, ministered with her sisters and brothers to thousands of the poor, and inspired the world in doing so, her inner life was desolation. She describes how she experienced abandonment by God, no consolation in prayer, and even what she dared to term the loss of faith.

I need to give only a single example so that those who have not read the letters might understand the desolation that she endured for most of her life and almost all of her ministry as foundress of the Missionaries of Charity. In early July, 1959, she wrote to her spiritual director, sharing her recent experience in prayer:

> Lord, my God, who am I that You should forsake me? The child of your love—and now become as the most hated one—the one You have thrown away as unwanted—unloved. I call, I cling, I want—and there is no One to answer—no One on Whom I can cling—no, No One—Alone. The darkness is so dark—and I am alone.—Unwanted, forsaken.—The loneliness of the heart that wants love is unbearable. Where is my faith?—even deep down, right in, there is nothing but emptiness & darkness.—My God — how painful is this unknown pain. It pains without ceasing.—I have no faith. — . . . If there is God,— please forgive me.[4]

The book's frontispiece carries a particularly affecting quote, one that in its profound shadow connects this servant of Jesus with the people of her age, those she served: "If I ever become a saint—I will surely be one of 'darkness.' I will continually be absent from Heaven—to light the light of those in darkness on earth."

These revelations from the woman's own heart shook the world's easy estimation of her sanctity. No

one can any longer rightfully claim that Mother Teresa
was able to do the amazing things she did because of her
great faith, or because of how close she must have felt to
God, or because of the great strength that feeling of near-
ness provided her. Her long experience was quite to the
contrary, and yet she stayed the course. She prayed for
others when prayer seemed to accomplish nothing in her.
She smiled when her heart was plunged into desolation.
She brought light to others while carrying the darkness
within herself. She preached in word and action the presence and love of Jesus while her own heart was crying
out for hours, months, and years for an encounter with
his love that would not come.

Did Mother Teresa merely exist here on earth? Did
she only survive? Some would say so. In my estimation
her life was a triumph of purpose, commitment, and
steadfastness of heart. This triumph is all the more true
against the somber backdrop of the inner life of pain she
bore. She brought fullness of life to many who had never
imagined it at all. She brought a sense of wholeness and
worth to the least among us. She could not have given
what she did not possess. Somehow, mysteriously, she
did possess the spiritual richness she shared with others.

What Athanasius and Mother Teresa Can Teach Us

Mother Teresa and the Patriarch Athanasius are just two
instances of what the gifts of groundedness and steadfastness in the Truth of Jesus Christ can do, have done,
and will do, in spite of all possible danger and difficulties
of this life and of all possible darkness and anguish of
the inner life.

In this day, with the faith we have, Jesus is saying to us all, "I have come that you may have life, and have it to the full." Our challenges in today's Church may be external, as were many of those Athanasius faced. They may threaten us with harm or ruin. Or the trials we face may be internal, as were the most intimate moments on the border of despair that Mother Teresa had to bear. Whatever we face individually or communally, there is good reason to hope that we can and will—as they did—do profoundly more than just survive. *Firmum est cor meum!*

NEXT STEPS

Prayer for a Steadfast and Unconquered Heart

Grant me, I beseech Thee, Almighty and most Merciful God, fervently to desire, wisely to search out, and perfectly to fulfill, all that is well-pleasing unto Thee. Order Thou my worldly condition to the glory of Thy name; and of all that Thou requirest me to do, grant me the knowledge, the desire, and the ability, that I may so fulfill it as I ought, and may my path to Thee, I pray, be safe, straightforward, and perfect to the end. Give me, O Lord, a steadfast heart, which no unworthy affection may drag downwards; give me an unconquered heart, which no tribulation can wear out; give me an upright heart, which no unworthy purpose may tempt aside. Bestow upon me also, O Lord my God, understanding to know Thee, diligence to seek Thee, wisdom to find Thee, and a faithfulness that may finally embrace Thee. Amen. (St. Thomas Aquinas, 1225–1274)

Lectio Divina

Remember your leaders who spoke the word of God to you. Consider the outcome of their way of life and imitate their faith. Jesus Christ is the same yesterday, today, and forever. Do not be carried away by all kinds of strange teaching. It is good to have our hearts strengthened by grace. . . . For here we have no lasting city, but we seek the one that is to come. Through him (then) let us continually offer God a sacrifice of praise, that is, the fruit of lips that confess his name. Do not neglect to do good and to share what you have; God is pleased by sacrifices of that kind. Obey your leaders and defer to them, for they keep watch over you and will have to give an account, that they may fulfill their task with joy and not with sorrow, for that would be of no advantage to you. . . . May the God of peace, who brought up from the dead the great shepherd of the sheep by the blood of the eternal covenant, Jesus our Lord, furnish you with all that is good, that you may do his will. May he carry out in you what is pleasing to him through Jesus Christ, to whom be glory forever (and ever). Amen. (Heb 13:7–9a, 14–17, 20–21, NAB)

Application

1. Research the date, place, and circumstances of your baptism. Prayerfully consider the significance of that key moment in your personal existence.

2. Think back to the darker moments of your life, when all seemed unfocused or lost; recall what carried you through to the light.

3. Consider the enormity of tumult and radical change that you have experienced personally and that we

have seen together. What will carry us through to victory?

Questions

1. Who are the grounded individuals who give you courage and inspiration in the practice of the faith given you in baptism?

2. Where are God's little ones, the poor on the periphery of your life?

3. Can you say with conviction, "Steadfast is my heart"?

4. If faced with the threat of having to renounce your faith in Jesus Christ, would you be open to offering your life?

NOTES

1. John Paul I, Address, October 15, 1984.

2. Tertullian, *Apologeticus*, Chapter 50.

3. Mother Teresa, Nobel Lecture, December 11, 1979, http://www.nobelprize.org/nobel_prizes/peace/laureates/1979/teresa-lecture.html (accessed February 27, 2014).

4. Mother Teresa, *Come Be My Light: The Private Writings of the Saint of Calcutta*, ed. Brian Kolodiejchuk (New York: Image, 2009), 186–187.

8.

BE INNOVATIVE IN A REVOLUTIONARY WAY

Joseph of Nazareth and Elizabeth Ann Seton

The Church is the original innovator. This should not be a surprise, as the Church's roots are found directly in the divine decision to send the second Person of the Trinity into the world incarnate, enfleshed, as a human being subject to suffering and ultimately to death. In other words, the Church is directly linked to the most innovative revolution that has or ever could occur.

And yet somehow over the past several decades the Church's public persona as presented via the major voices in news and commentary and cultural media has come to represent the very antithesis of innovation. The Church is often seen as the voice of antediluvian humanity, speaking for those who have noted no significant change in the world since before the Renaissance. The Church is portrayed as the last organization to recognize the equality of men and women and the final voice, besides that of Iran, opposing the existence of gays in the human family. In the press, the Church looks at best like the last living vestige of the early eighteenth century.

We must admit that Catholicism is not without blame in this situation. There are energies within the Church, sincere and hopeful, who see the way forward as primarily a continuation of what has been, of what worked in the past. The fact that many of Catholicism's best ideas lie in the past leads some to conclude that Catholicism's best days are behind us. Fearing that could be true, what can we do to prevent it?

The Church must do what she has done before and done more than once: embrace the fullness of the tradition and from its riches innovate, innovate, innovate. The only other option in this age of revolutionary change is to fade, to lose voice, to be sidelined and ignored by a greater and greater share of the population. Meanwhile, the media continues to communicate the Church's statements, in part out of long-time interest and respect, but also with an expectation that the opposing voices that are raised each time the Church speaks will make the real news.

Please note: my call for innovation is not a call to heterodoxy. When many voices speak from various viewpoints, all supposedly speaking for Christ and the Church, we create confusion and lessen the public sense that there is any real Christian voice. That is not innovation. Innovation is the renewal in the present of whatever has guided the Church in the past. What in the history of the Church has invited to faith, deepened life, and given hope to the suffering and dying? In the past, how did God join in conversation with the human family? In every age, particularly in a rapidly changing one like ours, innovation is the only way to maintain a steady, faithful, calm voice of faith and peace and to offer the invitation to salvation in God.

Because the Church of Christ is the original innovator, there is no need to simply adopt the concepts, technologies, and models that others have brought to light. It is fine and good to make use of Facebook and Twitter along with the old media of print, television, and radio, but the deeper innovation can and will come from within the life of the Church. Blending innovation and revolution, the Church can and will bring forth what we can call "innovolutionary" ideas that can both grasp the present moment and form the future.

In other words, Catholicism should aim for conception rather than mere adoption. Innovolution is the present interpretation of the tradition we receive and, at its base, of Jesus' own mandate. We need not fear, but rather need to feel called to innovate from the core to the skin. Again, this does not imply a change in teaching or doctrine. It does, however, mandate courageous shifts in terms of organization and presentation of what the Church believes and has to share with the world.

JOSEPH OF NAZARETH

Consider Joseph of Nazareth, husband of Mary and foster-father to Jesus. Go to the New Testament and read again the story of his betrothal to Mary, of her conception of the Child before they were married. Read as if for the first time, and put yourself in Joseph's position. How would you respond in his situation? Many times in the history of humanity there had been a pregnancy outside marriage. There were ways to deal with this predicament in the community of which Joseph and Mary were a part—though none of those ways were easy or pleasant.

All this was made more complex and overwhelming—infinitely more—because Mary said that the Child she carried was actually fathered by God. What would Joseph do? His world and his community had certain rules and expectations. Could he step outside the norms of his time and place? Would he have the commitment and the strength to allow the Spirit of God to lead him and his new family—geographically, ethically, spiritually—where they had never been before?

Or would he stay with the tried and true, ignore Mary's words and the strange dreams he was experiencing himself, and end the betrothal, leaving Mary and the Child without protection or place in the world? He could have done that. Most men in his situation would have done what was expected. But Joseph refused to leave Mary and the coming Jesus alone. He chose to join them in their aloneness. Together they were alone on the road to Bethlehem. They were alone before the anger, fear, and brutality of Herod. As a family alone, they fled on the refugee path to Egypt.

For millennia, the world has possessed the texts describing the hard moments and movements in Joseph's life. Churchgoers hear the narrative from year to year. It is good to step back to look and hear anew, with fresh eyes and heart, for that is exactly what Joseph of Nazareth was able to do. He looked at the unraveling events of his life with eyes and heart wide open. Joseph did not repudiate the tradition in which he lived. Rather he freely chose the most difficult option open to him, and in doing so transformed the situation (and so much since that moment) in unprecedented fashion.

In our time the Church needs to follow in the spirit of Joseph of Nazareth. Might we adopt Joseph as an innovolutionary patron now? Can we invoke his courage, openness, and commitment to respond in faithfully new ways to the moment in which we live?

Elizabeth Ann Seton

If we take these questions seriously, we can also take heart that others in their time have chosen Joseph's way of faithful innovation. Consider Mother Elizabeth Ann Seton. Elizabeth Ann approached a life filled with challenge and change with grace and flexibility that deeply characterized her sanctity.

Born a woman of wealth and privilege, she chose to depend on others to support the most important labors of her life. Nurtured and catechized in the Episcopal Church, she expressed her Christian faith most fully in the Roman Catholic Church. She was a wife and widow. She was a devoted mother, one who experienced the sad loss of many of her little ones in death while she survived. She founded a religious community and there became a mother in a new sense. She dared to step out into uncertainty to move from the places she knew well in New York to new territory for her in Maryland, and to establish there the first Catholic school in the nation. Strong and independent, Mother Seton was still able to team up with the Sulpician Fathers to make that foundation possible.

The litany of her accomplishments is long and impressive, but it may not leap off the page today. Imagination is an effective tool for putting ourselves in her place. Again and again in her life, what Elizabeth Ann Seton thought would last just passed away, disappeared from sight. Early on she might easily have stepped back out of the fray, out of the flow of life, out of public sight, and allowed her money to embrace her with comfort for the rest of her days.

Instead, she stepped forward again and again. With her life, energy, and talents, putting her mind, body, and spirit on the line, everything in Elizabeth proclaimed repeatedly, "Here I am, send me!" She may have expressed this willingness and commitment verbally, but more importantly she expressed it in the actions she took. At every major juncture she saw possibility where others saw no way forward. Mother Seton seemed to learn ever more deeply throughout her life that with God there is always a fresh way forward. An innovative solution is always possible, for in God all things are possible. He leads down a road of renewal that both respects and transforms the past.

WHAT JOSEPH OF NAZARETH AND ELIZABETH ANN SETON CAN TEACH US

Are we a Church worthy of the legacy of Joseph and of Mother Seton? In their times they had had reason more than once to be cowed and crippled by fear, to be slowed by confusion, to be halted by a sense that everything that could be done had been done, that everything that could be tried had been tried.

But they never did so. Theirs was a way that is recognizable, even from our distance in time and culture, as enlivened by the very life of the living God. But how do we recognize God's living way today? Where there are acrimonious divisions among believers on the "hot-button issues" of the day, where do we find the certainty that there is a way forward to unity and life?

What words describe that faithful new way? By whom are they spoken? And who shall recognize them for what they are—prophetic words? When we believers carry our disagreements right into the liturgical assembly, to the altar, to the Communion line, can we still yet believe that we are called to celebrate together, and do so with full hearts and open hands?

The innovolutionary stance we can take as a Church; the way that we organize ourselves to share the Gospel of Christ and to present Jesus' teaching and the tradition that flows from him—these can be, as they always have been, adjusted, changed, transformed. The Church has always done so to best carry out the commission given us by Jesus Christ, which still is ours today. As we open ourselves in faith to act as Joseph and Mother Seton, we need the voices, experience, knowledge, and talent of all who have ears to hear. No one is excluded.

If in our discouragement we step away from our call to teach and live the Gospel in our own time, we will fail our mission in Christ for our generation. But if we obey our call, cooperate with one another, and open ourselves to the Spirit's surprising directions, that will strengthen the Church in our day, bring joy to innumerable lives, and pass on a good example to those who will come after us.

NEXT STEPS

Prayer for an Innovative Spirit

Eternal God, in Whom we find not an iota of change: grant us a full measure of your creative Spirit. Your Son, the eternal Word, commissioned those close to him to make known the kingdom that is already here, but not yet. Nothing has changed in the urgency of that mission or the message has been handed down to us. By the indwelling of that same creative Spirit, allow us to see with clear eyes and a fresh heart the opportunities within our reach. Help us to actualize our inborn giftedness with imaginative and innovative outreach yet unapplied. Never let us forget that no inspired service, no matter how small, is without value. Hear our prayer right now for all those who are in a position to effect great changes and likewise for all those in a position to effect small changes for the good of your Church. Show us that we are never alone as we seek to obey your Son's commission to make disciples of all nations. Amen.

Lectio Divina

Now this is how the birth of Jesus Christ came about. When his mother Mary was betrothed to Joseph, but before they lived together, she was found with child through the holy Spirit. Joseph her husband, since he was a righteous man, yet unwilling to expose her to shame, decided to divorce her quietly. Such was his intention when, behold, the angel of the Lord appeared to him in a dream and said, "Joseph, son of David, do not be afraid to take Mary your wife into your home. For it is through the holy Spirit that this child has been conceived in her. She will bear a son and you are to name him Jesus, because he will save his people from their sins." All this took place to fulfill what the Lord had said through the prophet: "Behold, the virgin shall be with child and bear a son, and they shall name him Emmanuel," which means "God is with us." When Joseph awoke, he did as the angel of the Lord had commanded him and took his wife into his home. He had no relations with her until she bore a son, and he named him Jesus. (Mt 1:18–25, NAB)

Application

1. Reflect on the crippling effects of fear and confusion in your own past that have hindered your growth as a person and a disciple.

2. Identify what you consider to be the most outstanding, innovative act of your life and the effects of that act upon yourself and others.

3. List some frustrations in your personal, home, parish, or community life that your courage and creativity could change in a positive way.

4. Begin to search online, in publications, and around you for inspiring examples of people who are using their gifts to make a real impact in the life of the Church.

Questions

1. Consider the ministry of Popes John Paul II, Benedict XVI, and Francis. How did each of these men "reinvent" the ministry of Peter in their historical moment?

2. How have congregations of religious women and men had a deep impact on the spread of faith and the growth of the Church across the history of your country?

3. Who are the people in your life who have most inspired and influenced you by their creativity and zest for living their faith?

4. What are some of your "craziest" ideas for creating revolutionary change for the good?

5. Does your prayer ever beg the Holy Spirit for a previously unthought-of solution or a creative, even revolutionary, way to make disciples of others?

9.

BE READY FOR GOD'S SURPRISE

Patrick Peyton and Chiara Luce Badano

"Real friendship or love is not manufactured or achieved by an act of will or intention. Friendship is always an act of recognition."[1] The Irish poet, author, and seeker of wisdom John O'Donohue wrote those words in his first and best-known work, *Anam Cara*.

There is a profound truth here, and it's not only a truth about friendship. Blessings of all kinds, including the rich blessing of a friend, can and do spring up in unexpected places—as well as expected ones. A moment of grace is there in the silence following a summer rainstorm as well as in the sacred silence of a cathedral. The light of God's presence can shine in the eyes of an infant as they open after an afternoon nap, and just as truly in the closing eyes of a loved one dying. Athletic brilliance might shine vividly on a field of play during the Olympics, and similar brilliance can appear on a Little League field for those who have the eyes to see.

Sometimes we work hard to find the people and develop the capabilities, programs, and resources to strengthen something already in place or to initiate something new in the life of the Church. And that's fine. There is nothing wrong with planning well and working hard. There's nothing amiss in having a goal in mind and moving with determination toward it.

But there's this other truth we would do well to keep in mind and carry in our hearts all the time: God is free to act outside all our plans to make wonderful surprises happen. He is able to raise up men and women who astound us by who they are and what they are somehow able to do. In other words, in the parlance of our online and computer age: the rebirth of the Church is an open-source project. Sure, there are official efforts in the new evangelization going on all the time. There are appointed and anointed leaders who are working hard to inspire and move us forward. But there are also unexpected voices and surprising faces popping up like unbidden graces saying things like, "Look! This works too! We are making it happen over here like this."

New blessings are revealed every day, just as "his mercies are new every morning." The freedom of God's own Spirit, always present among the people of God, is seen in these surprises of grace that flow into the life of the Church in service to the world. These days a renewal of the Church has been announced and begun in Rome by the successors of the Apostle Peter. So we can expect God's abundant response to our openness to receive his gifts of rebirth. The look, the sound, and the feel of these godly gifts will be as diverse as are God's people.

PATRICK PEYTON

Look at the figure of Servant of God Father Patrick Peyton, the famed "Rosary Priest" who was a member of the Congregation of Holy Cross and a graduate of the University of Notre Dame. This son of the west of Ireland, who came to the United States to follow the call he felt to priestly ministry, found himself at death's door while still a young man. Praying the Rosary at this crucial moment, as he had been taught in his own home growing up in a family of faith, he was healed of tuberculosis, in his time almost always a death sentence. Not only did he survive, but also, in a sense, he found himself. His vocation, his hopes, and his plans all changed. None of them were any longer his own, as he might have thought them to be before his sickness. Everything from then on belonged but to God.

In 1942, in order to honor the Mother of God, Father Peyton began the Family Rosary by writing to every bishop in the United States and asking him to promote the praying of the Rosary by families at home in their dioceses. He felt called to undertake a crusade, first in the United States and then around the world, to encourage families and communities to pray the Rosary together. Father Peyton coordinated Rosary events in more than 40 countries, gathering more than 28 million people worldwide in the prayer of the Rosary. His influence has persisted for decades.

Recognizing the power of the media to touch families and society, Father Peyton founded Family Theater Productions in 1947, which produced over 900 radio programs, films, and TV specials. His mission, which continues today through the Holy Cross Family Ministries,[2] was to support the spiritual well-being of the family through prayer, especially through the Rosary. This servant of God gives us one of the best-known religious slogans of the twentieth century: "The family that prays together stays together." In those words, the Holy Spirit and Madison Avenue advertising meet, all for the glory of God.

No human authority, including any from the Church, called Peyton to this work, to this global ministry. The impetus came from beyond his ecclesiastical superiors. Peyton gathered crowds as large or larger than any pope before his time had ever gathered. Father Peyton's Cause for Sainthood was opened on June 1, 2001. He is known now as a Servant of God.

God has surprises in store for us. Always.

CHIARA LUCE BADANO

Blessed Chiara Luce Badano was a young member of the Focolare Movement who died of cancer in 1990 at the age of eighteen. Amazingly, ten years before, she wrote:

> One day you are born, no one asked you if you wanted to live. But now you are living. Sometimes it's nice for you. Sometimes instead you are sad. There are many things you don't understand. You are alive, but why are you alive? With your hands you must help to reorder the world. With your mind you must learn to distinguish good and evil. With your heart you must love people, and help them when you can. There are many tasks that await you. They await our hands, our mind, and our heart.[3]

On June 14, 1989, Chiara was admitted to the hospital in Turin. She had been experiencing a sharp pain in her shoulder which was causing her and her parents great anxiety. It was after consulting with the doctors that she

understood the gravity of her illness. She had been diag-
nosed with osteosarcoma, an aggressive form of bone
cancer for which treatment was limited. It was later that
same day she made up her mind that her entire life was
in God's hands. With this, her mother instantly noticed a
certain radiance in Chiara's face reflecting her deep trust.
That trust in God throughout her illness bore witness to
the faith already in her heart. She said at the time, more
than once, "Jesus, if you want this, I want it too."

This beauty and faith might have been silenced with
her death. But Chiara Luce's clear and bright witness
caught the attention of many, especially of young people;
not only in mind but also in heart. She was beatified in
Rome in 2010, and her cause for canonization continues.

Chiara and her family did not see her fatal illness
coming. Nor did the Church and world foresee the
power of her love of Jesus Christ, how it would continue
to touch hearts and grow in influence after her death.

WHAT PATRICK PEYTON AND
CHIARA LUCE BADANO CAN TEACH US

Chiara, like Father Peyton and so many others before
her, was, as we might say in television, a "live and
unscripted" gift of God. God does have surprises in
store. Not just in the past, but in our future. Not only do
we never know, despite all the wise prognosticators, who
the next pope will be, but also we never know the next
amazing marvel God will give to transform a moment
or an entire age.

We must seek out the leaders, ambassadors, entrepreneurs, and innovators among us, empowering lay
leaders and faith-filled professionals to dedicate their
skills to benefit the Church so as to invigorate the world

in every corner. Everyone has gifts to lend the Church as did Father Patrick Peyton and Chiara Luce Badano.

As you read these words, God's next surprise to lift up his people and to reveal the amazing grace of the Gospel is already happening. Our job is to keep our eyes open to recognize God's work. Is it happening right now within your own heart?

God is free, and powerful, and loving. We need never think that we understand God's ways.

But we certainly believe without understanding God's ways. As Saint Augustine used to say a millennium and half ago, "The moment you think you understand God, whatever you understand, that's not God." But understand this—this I believe: God is at work in Jesus Christ in the power of the Holy Spirit right now. And whatever God is doing, it is meant to transform our lives and to re-create his Church.

Next Steps

Prayer to Fit God's Plan

Creator God, Master of surprises, who am I that you would cast your gaze on me or ever think of me? Yet without your loving scrutiny and constant thought I would cease to be. You have made me wondrous from the moment your love first knit me together in my mother's womb. Now inspire me to look deep within this person you have created and sustained to do your work. Help me to fit my piece into the seeming puzzle of your harmonious plan. Likewise, help me to recognize in my brothers and sisters the giftedness that is theirs and how you are likewise at work in them for your glory. You create and redeem and sanctify us now and for eternity. Amen.

Lectio Divina

Meanwhile Moses was tending the flock of his father-in-law Jethro, the priest of Midian. Leading the flock beyond the wilderness, he came to the mountain of God, Horeb. There the angel of the LORD appeared to him as fire flaming out of a bush. When he looked, although the bush was on fire, it was not being consumed. So Moses decided, "I must turn aside to look at this remarkable sight. Why does the bush not burn up?" When the LORD saw that he had turned aside to look, God called out to him from the bush: Moses! Moses! He answered, "Here I am." God said: Do not come near! Remove your sandals from your feet, for the place where you stand is holy ground. I am the God of your father, he continued, the God of Abraham, the God of Isaac, and the God of Jacob. Moses hid his face, for he was afraid to look at God.

But the LORD said: I have witnessed the affliction of my people in Egypt and have heard their cry against their taskmasters, so I know well what they are suffering. Therefore I have come down to rescue them from the power of the Egyptians and lead them up from that land into a good and spacious land, a land flowing with milk and honey, the country of the Canaanites, the Hittites, the Amorites, the Perizzites, the Girgashites, the Hivites and the Jebusites. Now indeed the outcry of the Israelites has reached me, and I have seen how the Egyptians are oppressing them. Now, go! I am sending you to Pharaoh to bring my people, the Israelites, out of Egypt.

But Moses said to God, "Who am I that I should go to Pharaoh and bring the Israelites out of Egypt?" God answered: I will be with you; and this will be your sign that I have sent you. When you have brought the people out of Egypt, you will serve God at this mountain.

"But," said Moses to God, "if I go to the Israelites and say to them, 'The God of your ancestors has sent me to you,' and they ask me, 'What is his name?' what do I tell them?" God replied to Moses: I am who I am.* Then he added: This is what you will tell the Israelites: I AM has sent me to you. (Ex 3:1–14, NAB)

Application

1. God's plan for us, the Church, and the world is often surprising. List the three most surprising ways that God has been active and apparent to you.

2. Consider the saintly people in your life and experience. To whom have you tried to be a guiding, nourishing, encouraging presence, too?

3. Jesus made a solemn promise to remain with us always until the end of the age. Remind yourself over and over again of that promise, "I am with you," as a continual prayer of recognition throughout your day.

4. God has been and is even now mysteriously transforming you. Consider the ways you can better cooperate with God's amazing grace.

Questions

1. Am I actively looking for the glory of God in the many blessings and wonders of my surroundings and daily existence as and in the Church?

2. Who are the people in my family, parish, or circle of friends who need a push to service? How can I encourage them to see their giftedness and to spend themselves for the glory of God?

3. What is your most frustrating fault or shortcoming? How can you transform that into a kind of blessing, a means to powerfully transform your life and those around you?

4. Looking back over the totality of your life, what steps do you need to take moving forward to be more open and cooperative with God's grace working in and through you?

NOTES

1. John O'Donohue, *Anam Cara* (New York: Double-day, 1998), 22.

2. Holy Cross Family Ministries website, www.hcfm .org.

3. Pobal Parish website, www.pobalparish.com/ chiara.htm.

10.

LIVE WITH A
TRUE SPIRIT OF JOY

Teresa of Avila and Pope Francis

In John's Gospel we have words from Jesus that have brought hope to millions over the generations: "I have come that you may have life, and have it to the full." And later he says, "I have said these things to you so that my joy may be in you, and that your joy may be complete" (15:11). Saint John the Apostle and the Evangelist lived this full life, and through his letters he sought to pass that life onto the first generations of Christians. He explicitly states his purpose: "We are writing these things so that our joy may be complete" (1 Jn 1:4).

Full life. Joy. Complete joy.

This is what living life in Christ, in the Church, is meant to feel like. But think about it. How often do you turn to your neighbors in the pews around you at the sign of peace, look in their eyes, and see there the reflection of the experience of full life or of complete joy? You may see it on the faces of the very young, or perhaps the very old. In between, you are more likely to see evidence in those eyes of the burdens, worries, and cares that we are carrying through our days and years.

Think further of the people who likely number most of those whom you know: those who are not regularly part of the worshipping community at church from week to week, or who may not have any experience (at least in adulthood) of being a part of church. Is the fullness of life in them? Do you recall in conversations a sense that all they have hoped for in life is their experience now? Have you heard in their voices a consistent echo of joy? Not just of passing happiness, but of complete joy? Any joy at all?

Why is joy so lacking in the Church, in us Christians? If God became incarnate in Jesus Christ, spoke the Word of life to all, suffered and died in the flesh to take away the sins of the world, rose from the dead in unspeakable triumph, then commissioned his followers to tell the Good News to every people, and promised to be with us until the end of time—that is, if the creed of the Church is true—why is it so difficult to find joy in those who profess this faith? Where is the evidence among us of the gifts Jesus bestowed on us—full life, joy, complete joy? Instead, most of us exist most of the time in the mode of mere survival. Many have lost even the hope for fullness of life and complete joy. In this regard from those who do not believe the Gospel of Jesus Christ, we are often completely indistinguishable.

Perhaps it is too much to expect full life and complete joy. Yes, Jesus, the second Person of the Trinity, came and gave us many wonderful promises. Yes, the Spirit of God has been among us since the experience of the apostles at Pentecost in Jerusalem. But the reality in our own lives is that things are far from perfect.

The truth is that life is hard. The uncertainties of living, pain, sorrow, weakness, meanness and evil near and far, the sin within us, the plain old muck and muddiness of our days—these and a thousand other things teach us daily, even hourly, that, although Christ has triumphed gloriously, we have yet to share fully in that victory. Instead we are in the trenches of an ongoing battle. A child has brought the flu home from school, and now the whole family is sick. The marriage is strained. Money is short. And in the larger world we see actual wars being fought with many killed and wounded. We see hunger and disease. Many people have withdrawn into self to focus on personal gain and preservation of their wealth. So we may well wonder: in this broken world, how can I expect to do anything more than survive? Doesn't mere survival amount to success in the middle of this mess?

Perhaps we are right to embrace low expectations; perhaps we should even lower them further. Should we simply admit that our lives are always going to feel and be out of control?

Such resignation does not ring true as the rallying call of the disciple of Jesus. There must be another way. There must be a way that recognizes the kingdom that God is building among us. There must be a way of life that takes into account the often sad state of our world and yet is radically open to the gifts of full life and complete joy that we have been assured are to be ours. How can we live simultaneously on those two planes?

Perhaps we need a Year of Joy, a year during which we as Christians look for every possible reason to smile, for a smile can be magical. Picture the smile of a baby, the photograph of a child laughing with unbridled joy, or the transformed face of a sobbing person suddenly tickled by a wisecrack. Where does this smile come from? What does it mean? How is it attached to the soul?

In television or video production of any kind, a smile is often the first and strongest vehicle of the talent's projection. Psychologists and self-help professionals claim that a smile can actually heal physical and psychological ills; smiling is therapeutic. But beyond the secular, a smile is sacramental. The turned-up corners of our mouths can reveal the presence of Jesus Christ within us and the deep joy we find in sharing life with him.

Teresa of Avila

In the sixteenth century a saintly Spanish nun radiated joy in her smile and her wonderful sense of humor. As with any of us, Teresa of Avila had plenty of struggles and difficulties that might have made her somber or glum. She once cried out in prayer, "Oh, my Lord! How true it is that whoever works for you is paid in troubles!"

Teresa suffered tremendous physical pain. She was reported to the Spanish Inquisition; her plans to reform the Church both inside and outside were met with stiff resistance. Like many of us, she often found prayer to be a cold, seemingly one-sided conversation. And she was surrounded by pious, gloomy individuals. But none of this dampened her joy in being a child of God and a disciple of Jesus Christ. She is known to have prayed: "From sour-faced saints, Good Lord, deliver us!" Did the Lord smile at that?

Pope Francis

In the first year of his pontificate, during daily Mass in the *Domus Sanctae Marthae*, Pope Francis preached on the origin of our Christian joy. Smiling, he said this:

> We Christians are not so accustomed to speak of joy,
> of happiness. I think often we prefer to complain.
> [Instead, it is] the Holy Spirit that gives us joy: It's
> the Spirit that guides us: He is the author of joy, the
> creator of joy. And this joy in the Holy Spirit gives
> us true Christian freedom. Without joy, we Chris-
> tians cannot become free. We become slaves to our
> sorrows.[1]

The careful secrecy of a papal conclave makes it difficult to confirm, but there is a consensus of rumor that
in 2005 Cardinal Jorge Mario Bergoglio of Buenos Aires,
Argentina, was a serious contender to the papacy along
with then-cardinal Joseph Ratzinger. An anonymous
conclave diary leaked to the Italian media indicated that
the Argentinian cardinal received forty votes in the third
ballot, just before the man whom he would succeed to
the papacy was elected. That he was runner-up in the
previous conclave suggests to me that the Holy Spirit,
the author of joy, intends to use this Jesuit pope for the
"greater glory of God," the professed goal of all Jesuits
since Ignatius Loyola, their founder. I believe that the
greater glory of God is advanced by joy, like the joy of
the angel choir which sang to the shepherds at the birth
of the Savior, "Glory to God in the highest!"

An accomplished intellectual and a voice of con-
science to the whole world regarding the poor and mar-
ginalized, Pope Francis projects simplicity akin to his
namesake Francis of Assisi, the saint who aspired to the
humility and simplicity of Jesus himself. In our time
Pope Francis's quest for simplicity in his personal and
ministerial life seems unique. It inspires us. We are hop-
ing he can sustain it amid the strong traditions of pomp
and finery that attend the papacy.

Pope Francis first saw the light of day in Buenos Aires, Argentina, in 1936. The father of the first pope from the new world was an Italian immigrant and railway worker. The boy Jorge was one of five children. In 1958 Jorge Bergoglio entered the Society of Jesus and spent many of his early years teaching literature, psychology, and philosophy.

From 1973 to 1979, Father Bergoglio served as the Jesuit provincial in Argentina. As the Jesuit provincial, Bergoglio encouraged brother Jesuits to remain close to the people, ministering in parishes and as chaplains, rather than get involved in political activism or forms of ministry that would isolate them from people, particularly the most needy.

Jesuits are discouraged from receiving ecclesiastical honors and advancement, yet in 1992 Bergoglio was named auxiliary bishop of Buenos Aires, and then archbishop in 1998. In 2001, John Paul II appointed him a cardinal and assigned him the Roman church name after another Jesuit cardinal, Robert Bellarmine.

At a gathering of thousands of children from Jesuit schools in June 2013, Pope Francis was answering their questions when a touching moment ensued. A young redheaded girl no more than six asked Francis if he had wanted to be pope. After kidding with her a bit, Francis said flatly: "I didn't want to be pope."

Yet Pope Francis has admitted that he experiences a surprising serenity of soul and mind in the day-to-day exercise of the Petrine office. Since his parting words to the crowd in St. Peter's Square on the evening of his election (he said simply, "good night and rest well"), the infectious smile and humble demeanor of this good shepherd has proven attractive to Catholics, non-Catholics, friends of the faith, and even critics.

Pope Francis models a personal integrity and commitment to living the Gospel joyfully. He is in lock step with this "new evangelization" we hear and read so much about. In Francis, we see a credible call back to a personal relationship with Jesus Christ. From his first appearance in the white papal cassock to his many simple actions and genuine words, the pope makes clear one fact: "It's not about me. It's about Jesus Christ." His style of communication of baptismal faith is critical to our mission: he models to us the power of evangelizing selflessly with a smile!

A contemporary print of Jesus by artist John Tyler circulated far and wide in the 1970s. The pop-classic image depicted Jesus with a broad smile as if laughing at a hilarious joke. I wonder, how often did he smile? Was Jesus so deeply serious about his privileged relationship with the Father? Was he so weighed down in contemplation of his impending passion? Was he so aware of the past, present, and future sins of the human race that moments of pure joy were rare? I don't think so.

We need to see Jesus as he was. He was a happy man. His humble, compassionate, and authoritative person was so attractive that his presence gave people joy. I think of the aged, holy man Simeon, who, at the presentation of the infant Jesus in the Temple at Jerusalem, exclaimed, "Now, Master, you may let your servant go in peace, according to your word, for my eyes have seen your salvation, which you prepared in sight of all the peoples, a light for revelation to the Gentiles, and glory for your people Israel" (Lk 2:29–32, NAB).

During his ministry, Jesus invited the children to come to him. He named them role models for the rest of us. I have a movie playing in my mind of boys and girls flocking to him and laughing all around him, squealing with delight as he looked into their eyes, joked with them, and picked them up.

Jesus is the life of our party. If we don't respond to his attractiveness, we aren't really following him, no matter how much we profess religion or need it. The fact is that our religion, our faith, our message to the world is all about the Divine Person who took on our human nature and lived it to the full.

I am certain that Jesus had a beautiful smile. He still does. He is smiling at you and me right now. He is the most attractive person who ever lived. He was also the most joyful, even as he faced his horrible passion and death. He knew his Father's will was perfect, holy, and beautiful. He was delighted to play his part. He smiled a lot.

What Teresa of Avila and Pope Francis Can Teach Us

Teresa of Avila, a Doctor of the Church, knew that smile. She enjoyed a relationship with the Master that was deep and reverent, yet acknowledged his human nature. Once Teresa was thrown from her donkey as she travelled from one convent to another. When she tried to get up, she realized she had injured her leg. She prayed, "Lord, you couldn't have picked a worse time for this to happen. Why would you let this happen?"

And in her heart, Jesus said, "That's how I treat my friends."

Teresa replied, "And that is why you have so few of them!"

More than once, Pope Francis, speaking in his typical off-the-cuff style to a group of seminarians and novices in June 2013, took his listeners to task for being "too serious, too sad."

"Something's not right here," Francis said to the group. "There is no holiness in sadness." He noted that some Christians lack "the joy of the Lord. . . . If you find a seminarian, priest, nun, with a long, sad face, . . . it seems as if in their life someone threw a wet blanket over them."[2]

The pope's words apply to all of us, for joy is a powerful force in overcoming the daily challenges that life carries with it. Sorrow, pain, frustration, and setbacks can be real hindrances to our living as Jesus' disciples and being effective agents of the New Evangelization. Joy is one of the beautiful fruits of the Holy Spirit. When the Spirit of God comes to live within you, when you surrender to him, joy is yours.

Surrender to the joy of the Holy Spirit. Realize that you are one of those close friends of Jesus, even when you are thrown from your donkey now and again. Allow the joy of that friendship to show on our face! Jesus is smiling at you now.

And know that his promise to us is true: "I am with you always, until the end of the age" (Mt 28:20).

NEXT STEPS

Prayer for True and Lasting Joy

O God, Source of Life and all that is good, you know us and our weakness far better than we can know ourselves. Guide us to walk more readily in your ways. Help us to seek the values that will bring us lasting happiness in this changing world. Remove the things that hinder us from receiving Jesus Christ and expressing our joy in the resurrection of the Lord by the manner of our lives. We ask this through our Lord Jesus Christ, your Son, who lives and reigns with you and the Holy Spirit, one God, for ever and ever. Amen.[3]

Lectio Divina

I am the vine, you are the branches. Whoever remains in me and I in him will bear much fruit, because without me you can do nothing. Anyone who does not remain in me will be thrown out like a branch and wither; people will gather them and throw them into a fire and they will be burned. If you remain in me and my words remain in you, ask for whatever you want and it will be done for you. By this is my Father glorified, that you bear much fruit and become my disciples. As the Father loves me, so I also love you. Remain in my love. If you keep my commandments, you will remain in my love, just as I have kept my Father's commandments and remain in his love.

I have told you this so that my joy may be in you and your joy may be complete. This is my commandment: love one another as I love you. No one has greater love than this, to lay down one's life for one's friends. You are my friends if you do what I command you. I no longer call you slaves, because a slave does not know what his master is doing. I have called you friends, because I have told you everything I have heard from my Father. It was not you who chose me, but I who chose you and appointed you to go and bear fruit that will remain, so that whatever you ask the Father in my name he may give you. This I command you: love one another. (Jn 15:5–17, NAB)

Application

1. In your first thoughts and prayer each morning, recommit yourself to Jesus Christ and offer your whole day to him.

2. Be grateful for the good things in life, even if they seem overwhelmed by the difficulties you are experiencing at this particular moment. Focus more and more on the blessings you share.

3. Pray often during the day, even if for a few short seconds. Find a period of time and a quiet spot each day to turn over your burdens, most ideally before the Blessed Sacrament. You can't carry them alone.

4. Always keep the prize in sight: your goal is heaven! Living well this day is a step toward the life that is eternal.

Questions

1. What is it that makes you sad, long-faced, and unenthusiastic about life? How can you overcome and begin to remove these obstacles to joy?

2. Who are your models for joyful living? If you know them well enough, interview them about their joy in living.

3. What is the difference between patient endurance and a truly engaged life?

4. Who are the people living in the periphery of my existence? How can I help bring joy to their lives?

Notes

1. Pope Francis, Homily, May 31, 2013.
2. Pope Francis, Audience, July 6, 2013.
3. Drawn from various collects, *The Roman Missal*.

Father Robert Reed has long engaged television and new media for effective, entertaining, and truthful sharing of Catholic faith and life. A priest of the Archdiocese of Boston and the president of the CatholicTV Network, Reed was born in Boston and lives in West Newton. He was educated at St. John's Preparatory School and prepared for the priesthood at St. John Seminary College in Boston and the Pontifical North American College in Rome. Reed also studied broadcast administration at Boston University's School of Communication.

After being ordained a Catholic priest in 1985, Reed served in parishes in Malden, Norwood, Dorchester, Haverhill, and as pastor of Holy Ghost Parish in Whitman, Massachusetts. He was appointed to direct the CatholicTV Network in 2005. In addition to his administrative responsibilities at America's Catholic Television Network, Reed is also host of the game show *WOW: The CatholicTV Challenge*, and the reality series *House+Home*. He prays the Rosary with the television audience three times daily from various locations around the world; cohosts the network's signature talk show, *This Is the Day*; and celebrates daily Mass many times throughout the month. Reed also provides commentary for various national and international events from installations, ordinations, and papal liturgies.